Circle of Motion

*Arizona Anthology
of
Contemporary
American Indian
Literature*

Circle of Motion

**Edited by
Kathleen Mullen Sands**

Arizona Historical Foundation

Library of Congress Catalog Card Number:

ISBN: 0-910152-14-4 (Cloth)
ISBN: 0-910152-15-2 (Paper)

Copyright © 1990 — Arizona Historical Foundation
Tempe, Arizona 85287

Published in the United States of America

Illustrations by Adrian Hendricks
Book Design by Albert Camasto
Typeset by Ross Typesetting
Printed and Bound by Malloy Lithographing, Inc.

The paper used in this publication meets the requirements for
permanence established by the American National Standard for
Information Sciences "Permanence of Paper for Printed Library
Materials," ANSI Z39.48-1984.

Contents

Essays

Short Stories

Contributors

Preface

 It is the intention of this collection of poetry, essays, and short fiction to represent the landscape and contemporary life experiences of American Indian peoples in Arizona. While other anthologies have presented the creative literatures of specific tribes in Arizona or of tribal peoples in the American Southwest, no collection has focused directly on Arizona as it is known and experienced by American Indian writers. The works included here testify to the diversity and richness of tribal life in the state and to the creativity it has generated in the imaginations of American Indian writers.

While most of the contributors represented in the anthology are affiliated with Arizona tribes, many are from tribes outside the borders of the state. Because, like all Americans, contemporary Indians are highly mobile, and many of them have made their homes in urban areas or have taken up residence on tribal reservations other than their own, there are many Indian people from tribes which make their traditional homes outside of Arizona who either reside in or have spent time in the state. Because of this, we decided not to limit contributions to the volume to writers from Arizona tribes. As a result, many of the contributors are affiliated with tribes outside Arizona — Lakota, Gros Ventre, Chocktaw, Abenaki, Delaware, Cherokee, Mohawk, Creek, Seminole, Crow, Paiute, Oglala Sioux, Tuscarora, Kiowa, Koyukon, Ojibway, Cheyenne. What all the contributors hold in common and express in the work included in this volume is experience of the Arizona tribal life in the Arizona landscape.

Over 100 American Indian writers sent their poetry, essays, and short stories in response to our request for submissions. Selection of the works included in the anthology was based on four criteria: focus on Arizona landscape and tribal experience, diversity and balance in the genres and themes, the artistic quality of the work submitted, and limitations of space. We are sorry that more of the fine works that were submitted could not be included. We are particularly pleased that of the 34 writers represented, 23 are making their debuts as American Indian authors in *Circle of Motion: Arizona Anthology of Contemporary American Indian Literature*. All of the works in this volume are new; none has appeared elsewhere before being submitted for publication in this anthology.

It is our hope that *Circle of Motion* will speak with particular resonance to the American Indian people of Arizona and that it will reach out beyond state and cultural borders to generate appreciation for the creative expression of contemporary American Indian writers.

K.M.S.

Acknowledgements

I owe a sincere debt of gratitude to Dick Lynch, who, as Director of the Arizona Historical Foundation, initiated this volume and guided it to completion. Much appreciation goes to Allison Sekaquaptewa Lewis and Cynthia Wilson who served as editorial assistants throughout the work on the book, and to Adrian Hendricks who so thoughtfully and carefully conceived and executed the drawings to enrich the text. Thanks also to the staff of the Arizona Historical Foundation who supported the project throughout the process.

A special thanks to Joy Harjo for allowing the use of a phrase from one of her works, "Eagle Poem," in the title of the anthology.

To all those tribal people who submitted their work for the anthology, sincere thanks and encouragement to continue to share their experiences of American Indian life through their writing. This volume belongs to the contributors and to the tribal people of Arizona. It speaks for itself.

Kathleen Mullen Sands
Arizona State University

Introduction

Sonoran desert, high mesas, pine forests, rimrock, and deep canyons characterize the Arizona landscape. This is Indian country, a landscape where American Indian peoples have resided for centuries in isolated kinship groups, villages, tribal communities, and in modern times, in off-reservation small towns and rapidly growing urban centers. It is a landscape of traditions developed over centuries, of continuity with the past and harmony with the earth. But it is also a landscape of change, of movement between city and reservation, of immigration of Indian people from all over the country, of adaptation to a steady influx of non-Indian populations and growing environmental stress.

Circle of Motion represents the multiplicity of American Indian experience in the landscape that is Arizona. The circle is a symbol used by tribal peoples to represent the holistic and cyclical nature of life, the maintaining of traditional ceremonies and lifeways in harmony with the forces and rhythms of nature. It is the form that shapes much of the artistic expression of tribal people — pottery, baskets, beadwork motifs, architectural design — representing the sun and earth and the continuous repetition of nature. Motion, by contrast, is significant of change, of actions and events which take place in time. It gives vitality to the circle and generates adaptation of tradition to new phenomena and experiences.

The contemporary American Indian literature in *Circle of Motion* represents both tradition and change. It is local, focused on the part of the American Southwest that is delineated by the Colorado River, the tail end of the Rocky Mountains, and the border with Northwest Mexico. On this terrain live over 153,000 Indian people. Over 20 percent of the state's land is divided into 22 reservations belonging to the Navajo, Hopi, Maricopa, Tohono O'odham/Papago, Pima, Cocopah, Mojave, Apache, Yavapai, Havasupi, Kaibab Paiute, Yuma, Haulapai, Chimehuevi, and Yaqui tribes. Old Oraibi, on the Hopi Reservation, is the oldest continuously inhabited community in North America; the Yaqui village of Nueva Pascua near Tucson is the newest federally recognized American Indian community. Arizona is a landscape of the timeless and the timely, old ways being carefully nurtured and sustained alongside new ways of Indian living that are workable in the technological age. Arizona ranks third in the nation in Indian population and first in reservation population. Both Tucson and Flagstaff have large numbers of Indian residents, and Phoenix, the capital, has the sixth highest population of urban Indians in the country, indicating just how much movement has taken place among Indian peoples. Initiated by the historical removal of many tribal people from their traditional lands and the mid-20th century federal policy of relocating reservation Indians in urban areas, the percentage of American Indians now living away from reservations has risen above 60 percent. The mobility of contemporary Indians has infused the Arizona Indian population with tribal people from all over the United States. While tribal distinctions are strong and carefully maintained, many common themes and issues cross tribal boundaries to unite the Indians who are native to the Arizona landscape and those who have come here from other parts of the country either permanently or temporarily. The power to move between traditional and contemporary lifeways has been crucial to survival and continued identity and is a thematic thread that runs through this literature written about Indian life in Arizona.

Many of the poems in this collection recall the old ones, the Hohokam and Anasazi who came before. Images of petroglyphs on red cliff walls, pueblo ruins, bones, and pottery fragments attest to the ways of the people who dwelt on the land and vanished mysteriously before recorded history. One poet writes: "We have the ruins,/ a mound of plain/ clay pots, rude glyphs in rock,/sorrow for a culture's loss." The old ones speak to the present through the vestiges of their cultures and reaffirm the connectedness of present generations to the past and to the land. The writers remind us that the earth is mother to all living things, recalling mythic figures like White Shell Woman, Changing Woman, and Corn Mother as sources of power who generate ceremonies that honor women as bearers of culture and nurturers of families and the land. The poems are rich in images of corn, rain, pollen, sheep, sunrise, kivas, and chants.

But the connection between the mythic past and the present has not been seamless despite the continuity of ceremonies and stories. References to Kit Carson, General Carlton, broken treaties, ruthless betrayals, and cultural fragmentation figure prominently in many poems. A sense of historical displacement is often connected to threats to the land. Strip mining, jet planes, and missle silos contrast violently with images of cactus, rainbows, cottonwoods, and eagles. This dark realism is balanced by a sense of resiliency and by humor. Indian identity can be affirmed in a laundromat. Circle Ks, motorcycles, Dairy Queens, RVs, "Indian" beads made in Hong Kong, cheap bars and broken bottles, in the words of these authors, become part of landscape of Indian self-realization. Contemporary life is often a confusing collage of the tawdry and the reverent that leads to an ironic tone in many of the poems. Yelling

"Geronimo" gives a man the courage to leap into the sky and pull the parachute chord at the right moment. A lonely traveler watches "shakey dreams" in his rearview mirror. Lonely inheritors of a ruined world seek solace in the land and tradition.

Contemporary life is still connected to the earth. These poets write of enduring peoples. "Sudden laughter" fills the space where "only emptiness was," and "bodies become mountains" fused to nature in a deft gesture of metaphor that attests to the Indian poet's power to move toward renewal through language.

Correct movement on the earth and within tribal societies is posited on knowledge of the landscape and of kinship and traditional responsibilities which define the relationship of Indian peoples with the elements of the universe. That knowledge is gained through observation and through words; words put thoughts into motion. They express the unique relationship of the tribal person to place, tradition, community, and cosmos. *Circle of Motion* is an anthology of words. Through the language of a living landscape, these writers claim their place in the circle of tribal identity in Arizona.

The writers in *Circle of Motion* live in many cultures — traditional, contemporary tribal, mainstream American, urban, rural — often simultaneously. Their poetry, essays, and short stories reflect, not only the diversity of the Arizona landscape, but the multiplicity of cultures in Arizona and the spectrum of life styles and choices open to Indians today. Many of the words focus on movement, some of it physical — travelling across the state on freeways and back roads, moving through shopping malls, moving on foot through deserts and canyons, moving to the sound of ceremonial drums. Some of it is more act of imagination than physical motion — moving from one stage of life to another, moving toward a stronger sense of tribal identity. What unifies the works is that they themselves are moving, not only in the sense of depicting dramatic movement or development, but in the sense of affecting the reader. There is no artificial sentiment in the works in this volume, no vanishing Indian nostalgia. The writers are direct and passionate; they make the ordinary extraordinary through their language.

The language of the essays in *Circle of Motion* is closely connected to traditional storytelling in the sense that the presence of the teller is overt and the personal voice of the writer is felt. In each piece, the author speaks directly to the audience, in one case recollecting an amusing coyote story told by an aged uncle and its impact on the writer. In another, the author takes us into a peyote ceremony tipi to hear her grandfather talk to the participants about the stages of human life. We actually see him perform, shifting "the weight of his body to get comfortable" and leaning "forward a little." And we see his audience too, as they "stretch their legs," fix "loose hair," and wiggle from "side to side to relieve their backs." The oral tradition is brought alive as performance to which we become audience.

The literary strategy in the essays is both dramatic and meditative, incorporating philosophical viewpoints into description and story. The essay on coal mining at Black Mesa is a clear warning of the consequences of disrespect for the land, but it is not a political diatribe. It places a contemporary problem within the framework of traditional storytelling, describing the mining machinery in terms of the evil giants who roamed the Navajo world in the mythic past, and depicting the contemporary environmental abuse and the need to eradicate it in terms of an ancient pattern of threat and recovery.

The sense of a personal or family past is also strong in this section. Two of the authors share episodes from their childhoods. A sense of "being there" characterizes this technique, much as it does in the storytelling format of the other essays. Recollection of a young Yaqui girl's companionship with her father as he irrigates the cotton fields is written in the present tense. The time between the writer's adulthood and childhood is collapsed, and as readers, we are there too, moving across the flooded field, "smelling the damp eareth and the wet desert plants," digging "toes in the mud, sailing little twigs in the ripples of the water."

Moving correctly in the contemporary world is not easy. The conflict of competing cultures often causes breakdowns in personal relationships and isolation from traditional structures of tribal knowledge. Sometimes the circle is shattered and motion is hesitant or ineffective. For many contemporary Indians, correct movement must be worked out on an individual basis and the risk of failure is heightened with increasing pressures to act according to the norms of the dominant culture. The literature of *Circle of Motion* depicts the dilemmas of modern life for Indian people. It addresses the issue of retaining tribal identity in a world generally at odds with the natural cycles of time and unconcerned with the survival of traditional ways. Grinding poverty, environmental abuse, family break-ups, alcoholism, discrimination in the legal system, the trauma of returning veterans, and loss of tradition are all part of the Arizona Indian experience. The realism with which these writers deal with the darker side of Arizona Indian life is disturbing. They challenge some of the simplistic but nonetheless popularly touted stereotypes about the "nobility" of native peoples. Continuity with the past, reaffirmation of Indian values, even basic survival, is sometimes impossible in the works presented here. Expectations are modest; the memory of broken promises and broken dreams is too raw to admit soaring hopes. The writers are painfully honest about desperation and dispair.

The short stories collected here offer a somewhat grimmer view of Arizona Indian life than the other genres in the volume. There is comedy, but it's more bemused and ironic than hearty because it is framed in serious circumstances and elucidates cross-cultural misunderstanding, as it does in the story about the flight of two Indian convicts who know they will be caught but are determined to perform the sweat bath the prison chaplain denies them. The return to prison looms before them and mutes the humor for the reader.

In another story a man finds himself prevented from holding onto the child of his former lover despite the father-daughter bond they have developed. He is too Indian; she is too fair, and no blood ties bind them, so they are wrenched apart. The bedtime story he tells her, with its promise of "happily ever after" offers a wry sort of wit by contrasting the fairytale world with reality. Fairytails don't come true in real life and running away to the woods cannot reunite the man and child. Even a simple love story has a sad tone. The relationship is tenuous — an absent husband shadows the warmth of their passion and partnership — and there is a tempering of emotions between them.

The love between generations — father and daughter, grandmother and grandson — is poignantly depicted in two stories. In one, the grandmother of Indian traditional stories — respected and cherished — is replaced by the modern day elder who has raised her grandson selflessly and carefully but loses him to war and alcohol. In the other, an old man, afraid of losing his daughter's care, gives up his beloved pet birds. Even in a story that concentrates on childhood in a loving traditional family, the child's confusion and fear at the trading post is palpable as he tries to cope with the strange manners of the whitemen who stare at him and talk too loud.

Modern life on the reservation or in the city is often temporary and fragmented, these short story writers say. There is little to hearten the spirit unless one turns back to the land and to tradition.

The general tenor of *Circle of Motion* is not, however, pessimistic. Despite the historical record of injustice toward tribal people and the contemporary burden of conflicts that they carry, Indian people do survive. In Arizona, as elsewhere in the nation, they hang on tenaciously to their lands and foster their cultural identities through ceremonies and by passing stories and songs from old to young. At the same time tribes are working hard to ensure survival of their languages, many of their young people are learning to express the complexity of tribal cultures in English for both Indian and non-Indian readers. The writing in *Circle of Motion* clearly demonstrates that knowledge of and respect for traditional ways is not disappearing, and that there are many Indian writers, experienced and new, who are compelling in their use of genres of literature in English. It also recognizes the complexity of contemporary Indian life and the variety of responses to it within the Indian communities of Arizona. From place to place, from tribe to tribe, from individual to individual, the experience of being Indian in Arizona is both unique and shared. And so it is that Arizona is a rich landscape for literature by Indian writers. *Circle of Motion* is a celebration of those Indian voices and of Indian life in the landscape that is Arizona.

Kathleen Mullen Sands
Arizona State University

Poetry

Colors of Bones

by Avis Archambault

I dream of colors
that
    blind men see
BRILLIANT   like SUN
unseen   but
felt —
    like I Feel,
feeling rainbows that strike
MOTHER EARTH   and bounce back
like
    an arrow,
to pierce a   single   frail
cloud
    over Salt River   as
THUNDER-BEINGS,   speaking   in
stages
    shatter the
dusky obsidian sky,
    leaving
broken stars   like
ANCESTOR'S BONES,
        RED bones —
BRILLIANT   like SUN
and like
COLORS
    that blind men see.

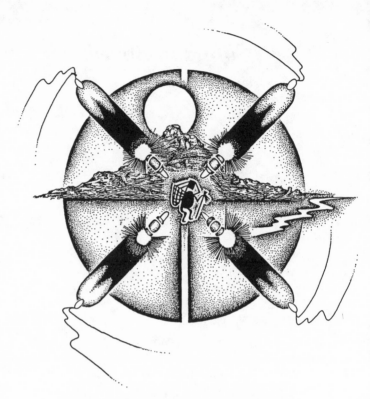

Our Circle of Women /
and Grandmother's Eagles

by Avis Archambault

Dawn / The Power of
The Woman
lights the Eastern quarter;
deer-like, running the
edges of 'Red Mountain'
toward Neva's house
still dreaming under
Owl's protective wing, as
first light lengthens
shadows behind the
Sweat-lodge.

4

Face lifted / eyes closed
she stands between
Mountain Mystery and
River Power; who
always agree to meet
in Neva's backyard
just like other passing travelers.
NEVA —
Solidly rooted in the
calmer depths of
Salt River / her prayers
seeping out to
              distant paths of the Reservation.

First light
catches pipe-stone warmth
through the trailer window.
BEA —
washing her hair with
morning prayers / steps out
to offer her Lakota song;
     "Friends, this is the way,
      Friends, this is the way," as
small winged-brothers brightly agree
carrying the message in
Four directions /   returning
to find room
          in the bowl of her Pipe.

EARTH FEATHER tends her
early morning garden,
strength, daily growing with
her plants and prayers / treasures
this little time for self.
Soon
the children will burst forth
like some other sunrise;
pouring their needs over
this young Mother.
She has learned the Wisdom of the willow;
branching the distance   from husband to child
to the land,   to her People
Softly
       bending in many directions.

Across Pima road,
One dances the Dawn —
to honor Tolteca — The Aztec past,
AVIS —
who walks, a
foot in both Worlds
holds tight,
her drum   and Eagle feather!
"Wazia!" she calls
facing the North to dream of
The Mountain and distant relations,
to dream of the Mountain where
she'll offer her Dance,   her prayers
her Life
for all her relations
                    And Grandmother's Eagles.

Sunrise sees
MONA —
who lives to the South,
rich in Kindness   and Generosity
standing beside   or
behind her
Strong man,
offering   prayers
prayers   like jewels
for her many   sisters
MONA
always   able for
                    ALL Love requires.

Morning Star reflects last light
through crystal   held,   by
She-the-Elder   Keeper   of
Grandmother's Eagles.
ELOISE —
who lives to the West
her rightful place,
the place   of Power

LIFTS
the crystal   to see   star-clear;
prisms   that
dance
disappear,
reappear —
that swirl   and spiral
                    Uniting Our Circle of Women
watching:

Dawn / The Power of
The Woman
light the Eastern quarter;
deer-like,   running the
edges of   'Red Mountain'
                            towards
                            NEVA'S house

Sandhills That None May Visit

by Aroniawenrate / Peter Blue Cloud

Sandhills that none may visit.
Crumbled ruins which echo a song
carried on the winds of yesterday.
A lone coyote keening the moon,
the headlights of a car
    searching thru the night.
The silent laughter of stars
as they dance their light
across an endless landscape.

Each daylight rises, a praise
in the song of Creation.
A circle of drummers and singers
gathered low upon a sandhill,
and the eagerness of ourselves
in a running stagger thru sand
to join their circle.
          And they
keep fading back into distance,
and their music is like a memory,
as we become shadows of tomorrow
on the red stone cliffs of today.

Springtime flowers born of snow,
crystals floating on a desert wind.
A sacred message etched in sand,
magic tumbling tracks of sidewinder.
At the corner of the eye, naked stone,
and lightning dancers leaping from
black, rumbling storm clouds.

A large track no one recognizes
    behind us,
slowly filling with sand.
Sudden laughter where
    only emptiness was.
A lizard transfixed upon a stone
waiting into forever,
          as we
do pushups and grow tails.

Dried, scattered corn stalks
rustling in the desert wind
    as an old man
shakes a gourd rattle and chants,
his eyes closed, a smile playing
games of youth.
A woman on her knees, patting
soft circles of frybread
    as a child
watches her, and then solemnly
says, "I'm going to be a dancer."
And the woman looks back
at the child as solemnly
and says, "Yes, you will be a dancer."

A piece of pottery, smooth and
rounded by fingers of wind,
the same wind whose flute plays
the cottonwood's Creation song.

We pass our own scattered bones
lying in jagged fragments,
home for scorpions,
              and we
smile at those brittle memories,
crumbling them between fingers.

And we pause at a waterhole
to study the countless markings,
and drink deeply, to become rivers,
and lie back upon the sand
and stretch out, and out,
as our bodies become mountains
and crumble into sandhills
    that none may visit.

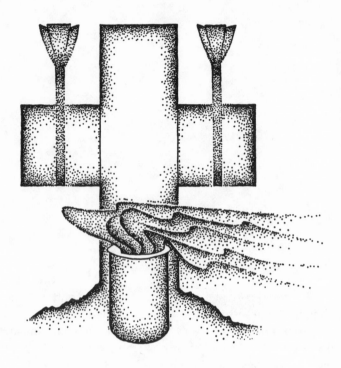

Postcard to Kaz from Somewhere South of Allah

by Jim Barnes

Dear Kaz, I miss the crosses by the roads
that made me slow before. They took them down
I guess to lure retirees home to Love
and other places needing cash never
seen before. I crossed the Prescott range
at dusk to wonder if that steely sun
consumed somebody's reservation north
of Blythe. The altitude allows wonders.
I know why Cochise fought. I drive too fast.
At Allah I had to rest the Mustang
and my face. All the way from Gallup I've tried
to remember my one-time schoolboy tally
of white crosses for those who never made it.

Blue Coyote

by Joseph Bruchac

Sonora

First Maker walked
and where he went
each step became a living thing.
He walked through thorns,
left horned lizards behind,
walked through colored sands,
Gila monsters were there.

With a piece of flint
on the cliff of blue stone
he drew a shape —
lean with four legs,
a head always looking
back over its shoulder
its tail a breathing wind.

Then, quick as an arrow released from a bow,
it leaped from the cliff
right up into the heavens.

Now, when night sky is clear,
do you have to ask
whose bright eyes
look down into your dreams?

Pima Scenic Outlook

by Joseph Bruchac

The cactus wren
cocks its quick silver eye
at my strange face
on the piled stone peak.

Below, in the flatlands,
Old Tucson wavers,
a drowned city's mirage
in the tourist sun.

Cars and campers
from a dozen states glitter,
Hong Kong beads strung
on the thread of road.

Few stop to look
at the lines of cactus,
saguaros climbing hills
like old women and men.

Long after we've gone,
they'll hold these slopes,
finding earth's deep moisture
with patient roots.

The New Moon

by Marvin Cling

The evening red sky turns purple.
The sun hides, another day fades.
Near and full, white like my coat,
Is the moon, then it is night.

A two-legged wolf I become,
Then I seek near-by hogans.
For an evening's tale, I cast a spell.
At the brow of the canyon, I howl.

Truth is medicine man's lore.
In my mind, the wind whispers a chant.
From resting places, I hear pleas.
An owl flies to nest, a coyote cries to rest.

Soon the sun comes, then a singer I become.
Then I heed to someone in need.
Songs, herbs, pollen make the ill pure.
Until the new moon, I heal and sing.

Full of legends is the ceremony.
I speak of those who haunt the living,
Deal with the dead, the dark beings.
A dead one's spirit causes the illness.

With the lore, my song continues.
A wolf howls for the day to fade.
A singer prowls to complete the rites.
Until the new moon, no more lures.

Perception

by Benjamin Cooley

The sun, father
    Our protector and guide
From you, life flows

Land, mother
    Our birth and strength
From you, life begins

The rain, brother
    Our refresher of the air
From you, life continues

The rainbow, sister
    Our artist of the waters
From you, life's beauty seen

The stars, relations
    Our heavenly guardians
From you, life's perfection.

Trading Posts

by Dan L. Crank

Old, rickety, stone buildings.
Cottonwood trees bare; broken bottles
    gleam in warm sun.
Lone Indian stands under winter tree, hands
    deep in pockets.
An old Navajo man, wishing for a companion.
    Someone like him, from the past days.
To reminisce about when Trading Post was new.
    Back in heyday when Post was bustling.

Used to walk in with something to trade.
The brighter, the bigger, the better.
    So other Navajos present will envy.
    So it will be news for about a week; this week's hero.
Also good to confront Trader (almost touching, sometimes
    daring to tug at his shirt).
And demand a good deal.

Now, plastic, shining buildings.
    Neon signs flashing out new names.
    Not Trading Post, but Circle K, 7 to Eleven, Thriftway.
Also, clean, tar paved streets.
If you're a lone Navajo, and you stand outside for longer
    than five minutes; others wonder about you.
Are you begging for money, or are you hitchhiking?

Coke cost ten cents; candy bar, a nickel.
Skoal was twenty-five cents and gas, nineteen cents a gallon.
    With a dollar, you had a good time.
In Trading Post, leaned against counter.
    Checked mail once in awhile; bought a coke every thirty minutes.
Watched, commented on other Navajos' purchases.
    Laughed at and with others.

Trader didn't mind you standing in store
    for a length of time.
In fact: Trader knew you by first name, and you exchanged news.

Ancient buildings now in only a few places, like Oljato (Moon Water).
    Wooden counter that you leaned on still there;
    some initials from past almost worn out completely.
Once, a laughing place, a good trading place, and a place
    of commotion.

Trader (with an earned Navajo name) knew
    your family.
Once, Trader was your friend, your letter-writer, your interpreter;
    and someone you trusted.
Today, group of Navajo teenagers outside
    Circle K, wondering where to go, and what to do.
Their modern Trading Post is an alien, quick place.
Trader don't even know you.
    Trader only want your money.
If you stand outside too long, they call the Navajo police.

Medicine Man

by Jefferson L. Curtis

The medicine man sits in his shack
while the sands glisten in the sun
others sing in the background
he starts to make his design
he says it depends on what the problem is
now he's finished and we can go home.

Changes in the Rocks

by Eagle Feather / Ray Begaye

Awake, look, listen, hear
the ants are dancing
in the valley lo
the red ants are dancing
atop Lok'agigai
they are dancing in rhythm . .
on top of the rocks.

Awake, for they are dancing
from the reach of the valleys
from the lift of the mountains
for they are dancing in rhythm . .
with the changes in the rocks.

(1974)

By Any Other Name

by Raven Hail

Geronimo! came the savage yell,
As the brave young paratrooper fell.
His parachute opened, full and round,
And swung him safely to the ground.

Why do you say 'Geronimo'?
The Old Apache wanted to know.
You've got it wrong, this word you say —
His name was really Gokhlayeh.

The youth replied: I need a word
That gives me time to pull the cord.
Before I could say — what you just said,
I'd hit the ground and end up dead!

Bird

by Joy Harjo

The moon plays horn, leaning on the shoulder of the dark universe
to the infinite glitter of chance. Tonight I watched Bird kill himself,

larger than real life. I've always had a theory that some of us
are born with nerve endings longer than our bodies. Out to here,

farther than his convoluted scales could reach. Those nights he
played did he climb the stairway of forgetfulness, with his horn,

a woman who is always beautiful to strangers? All poets
understand the final uselessness of words. We are chords to

other chords to other chords, if we're lucky, to melody. The moon
is brighter than anything I can see when I come out of the theatre,

than music, than memory of music, or any mere poem. At least
I can dance to "Orinthology" or sweet talk beside "Charlie's Blues,"

but inside this poem I can't play a horn, highjack a plane to
somewhere where music is the place those nerve endings dangle.

Each rhapsody embodies counterpoint, and pain stuns the woman
in high heels, the man behind the horn, beats the heart.

To survive is sometimes a leap in madness. The fingers of
saints are still hot from miracles, but can they save themselves?

Where is the dimension a god lives who will take Bird home?
I want to see it I said to the Catalinas, to the Rincons

to anyone listening in the dark. I said, let me hear you
by any means: by horn, by fever, by night, even some poem

attempting flight home.

Eagle Poem

by Joy Harjo

To pray you open your whole self
To sky, to earth, to sun, to moon
To one whole voice that is you.
And know there is more
That you can't see, can't hear
Can't know except in moments
Steadily growing, and in languages
That aren't always sound but other
Circles of motion.
Like eagle that Sunday morning
Over Salt River. Circled in blue sky
In wind, swept our hearts clean
With sacred wings.
We see you, see ourselves and know
That we must take the utmost care
And kindness in all things.
Breathe in, knowing we are made of
All this, and breathe, knowing
We are truly blessed because we
Were born, and die soon within a
True circle of motion,
Like eagle rounding out the morning
Inside us.
We pray that it will be done
In beauty.
In beauty.

Healing Animal

by Joy Harjo

On this day when you have needed to sleep forever,
to forgive the pained animal kneading
                            your throat.
Sleep, your back curled against my belly.
I will make you something to drink,
                            from a cup of frothy stars
from the *somewhere there is the perfect sound*
called up from the best stories
                            of benevolent gods,
who have nothing better to do.
                            And I ask you,
what bitter words are ruining your soft skinned village,
because I want to make a poem that will cup
                            the inside of your throat
like the fire in the palm of a healing animal. Like,
the way Coltrane knew love in the fluid shape
of a saxophone
                    that could change into the wings of a blue angel.
He tasted the bittersweet roots of this crazy world,
and spit it out into the center of our musical
                                        jazzed globe.
Josiah's uncle brought his music
            to the Papago center of the world
                            and music climbed out of his trombone
into the collected heartbeat of his tribe.
They had never heard anything like it,
                    but it was the way they had remembered, the way
"Chief" Russell Moore must have known when he sang
                                        for the very first time
through the brass-boned monster.
All through the last few nights I have watched you fight for yourself
with the eyes I was warned against opening.
                                    You think you are asleep
when you turn off the lights, and we blend into the same
                            hot-skinned sky.

The land called miracle is the daughter you never died for and she
stands at the edge of the bed with her slim hand
                                        against your cheek.
Your music is a crystal wall with a thousand mouths, kin to trains and
sounds that haven't yet been invented
                                        and you walk back and forth
through it to know that it won't betray you.
And in the last seconds before the breaking light
when you are nearly broken with the secret antelope
of compassion,
                    when the last guardian angel has flown west to the Pacific
to see someone else through their nightly death,
a homefire is slowly kindled in the village of your body.
And the smoke of dawn turns all of your worded enemies
into ashes that will never rise.
Mythic cattle graze in your throat, washing it with milk.
And you will sing forever.

(for L.N. and Michael Harper)

Javelina

by Joy Harjo

The sun falls onto the bristly backs of foraging javelina west of the desert
oracle and the soft streets stiffen with crawling dark. I drive South Tucson.
I am the one standing at a pay phone with a baby on her hip, just 17.
Do I need a job? Has the car broken down again? Does the license plate say
Oklahoma? I travel from a tribe whose name bears storm clouds, and have
entered a land where a drink of water is a way to pray. I was born of a blood
who wrestled the whites for freedom, and I have since lived dangerously in
a diminished system. I, too, still forage as the sun goes down: for lava
sustenance. The javelina know what I mean. I can no longer imagine this
poem without them, either their ghostly shapes of light years reversed, or
the tracks now skating behind them in the sand.

I want to stop the car, and tell her she will find her way out of the soap
opera. *The mythic world will enter with the subtlety of a snake the color of
earth changing skin. Your wounded spirit is the chrysalis for a renascent
butterfly. Your son will graduate from high school. You have a daughter not
yet born, and you who thought you could say nothing, write poetry.*

And would she believe me?
And does she now?

Her husband comes out of the cheap room with more change and a coke. I
cannot turn my head or lie; it has gotten me nowhere. I leave her there. But
for years I pray for rain, for her beaten spirit to lift up and rain and rain.
The cicadas enter with a song at the torn edge; they call forth the burning
sunset the color of the lips of the unseen guardian of mist. A renegade
turtle hides beneath damp runners of a plant with red berries; tastes rain. I
imagine the talk of pigs and hear them speak the coolest promise of spiny
leaves. Their prevalent nightmare has entered recent genetic memory, as the
smell of gunpowder mixed with human sweat.

I have done time on their streets, said an elder with thick tusks of wisdom.
*And I understood this desert without them. It is sweeter than the
blooms of prickly pear. It is sweeter than rain.*

We Encounter Nat King Cole As We Invent the Future

by Joy Harjo

Camme and I listened to Nat King Cole and she sweetly lay her head
on the shoulder of some well-slicked man and off
she went some slow easy step some 30 years ago it wasn't
yesterday but ghosts of time in tilted hats are ushered
by our heartbeats into the living room as we eat fried chicken,
drink cokes and talk about swing, don't talk
about heartbreak but it's in the stirred air. How we loved,
and how we love. There is no end to it.
One song can be a crack the whip snapping everything
we were in the lifetime of a song back
into the tempest of dreams. And when the cokes are gone,
chicken bones drying in the sun,
radio shifted into another plane of time I don't know
what to believe. My heart's a steady tattoo of roses.
Camme and I go to sleep in our different houses, she without
her dancing man, and me with my imaginary lover
outlined in smoke, coming up the road. There's a song
that hasn't been written yet, the first notes
are a trio of muses in a songwriter's ear. That song will invent
my lover of evening light, of musky genius,
I know it. As sure as I know Nat King Cole wore white suede
shoes, and smelled like spice hair creme,
as sure as the monsoon rains come praising the dry Sonoran.
Yesterday I turned north on Greasewood
the long way home and was shocked to see a double rainbow
two stepping across the valley. Suddenly
there were twin gods bending over to plant something like
themselves in the wet earth, a song
larger than all our cheap hopes, our small town radios,
whipping everything back
into the geometry of dreams: because Nat King Cole
became the sultry blue moon became all
perfumed romantic strangers became Camme and I
became love
suddenly

25

My Aunt Ponders Her Widowhood

by Lance Henson

late summer
on the san carlos reservation
there is little to do
booze and hunt peridot
look for work

the mountains have not forgotten their task
they stand in bare sunlight
offering what vision the sky has not worn away

just after dawn my aunt sits near the window
a smoking cigarette and a cup of coffee
on the table
she has not grown use to the silence
the footstep that never quite sounds

there is a little wind on the curtain
about the size of a mouse's* breath

hear it

it brushes my aunt's cheek
and she smiles

---

*my uncle's nickname

This Is No
Arizona Highways Poem

by Lance Henson

(on the journey to bury my uncle)

mid afternoon
driving through globe
my sister drunk in the back seat naming all
the bars the skins* hang out in

after passing the san carlos apache
reservation
i watch shaky dreams made of rain
in the rearview mirror

pulling into a station for gas
the wipers create a surreal picture
of this city

my mouth cotton dry after driving non stop
from oklahoma

we are just indians lost in the blur
of america

and again

we have come to bury our dead

---

*term for indians

Hopiland

by Inoj / Joan A. Torralba

I am here
As I have always been.

A land of beauty and mystery
I am blessed.
I am tended by my flock
I am father, I am mother.

The sun is my smile
The wind my exhilarance
The rain is my nurture
The snow my white hair.

I am here
As I have always been.

For I am ageless
My face has many crags
Here time has no meaning
My years make no difference.

My children revere me
My strength will never fail
I will be forever
Beyond the end of time.

I am here
As I have always been.

A Navajo's Song of Life

by Genevieve Jackson

House God my grandfather calls to me,
"Rise my child, breathe the spirit of life."
At dawn, I run and listen for the White bird's call.

I welcome Sun Bearer. Corn pollen
I sprinkle. With Beauty beneath me, beauty
before me, beauty following me
and beauty above me, I greet the day.

White Shell Woman, my mother caresses my face.
"My beloved child, embrace life.
Treat your brother with honesty, share your
goods. Do not judge and speak ill of your
neighbor."
Variegated goods I offer.
Jet, black like her hair.
Turquoise, for the beads that adorn her,
Abalone, the color of her dress.
White Shell Woman, Mother of Monster Slayer
and Borne of the Water, Mother of the Navajo Nation.

Talking God, traveling on Black wind into the yellow twilight,
Summon the dark clouds and Male rain.
Replenish White Corn Boy and Yellow Corn Girl for your children.
Grandfather, guide me through life. Retain in me
a love and respect for Mother Earth.
As you descend into your western home and
Evening Light Boy and Abalone Girl steal across the
land, soothe my brows, erase my fears.

Black God (Haschezhin), Fire God, Grandfather,
adorned with blue turquoise,
Guardian to the South on Mt. Taylor
Restore harmony to my soul.
Voyaging on the blue wind, bring the soft
gentle, female rain to succor
the creatures of Mother Earth.

Monster Slayer, twin of Borne of the Water,
destroyer of Evil spirits,
Help me maintain balance with all living things.
Teach me to respect the elements of life; Fire, Water,
Wind and Mother Earth.
Fearless warrior, Sentinel of Dibentsaa,
May my feet never travel past the four sacred mountains.

When my eyes grow dim and Mother Earth
readies herself to receive me, I will say:
"In Beauty it was planned. In Beauty it was begun.
In Beauty it was done. In Beauty it will be evermore.
Hozho'nagasglii, Hozho'nahas glii, Hozho'nahas glii,
Hozho'nahasglii."

Belly Button Blues

by Geri Keams

i thought of all our belly buttons
where they were buried
on the land near winslow
i thought of all nine belly buttons
grandma said it was part of the old ways
they buried your belly button in the
sheep corral if you were a boy
and under the house if you were a girl
well . . mine got lost in a suitcase
that's why my mom says
i'm always travelin' and
maybe never settle down
i call it the belly button blues.

Broken Peacepipe

by Geri Keams

One time, he said, in the old days . . . when the old ones
were ready to leave Fort Sumner . . . when the peace treaty was to
be signed. All the Navajos were anxious to go home. They had
been in something like a concentration camp for four years and
now finally they were ready to sign the 1886 peace treaty.

General Carlton . . . I think that was his name . . . he said he
wanted to show Washington that he was finally going to get the
Navajos civilized and that they were going to settle down and
herd sheep. Carlton was all excited about the signing of the
peace treaty. Always, Bob said, Carlton wanted to smoke a
peacepipe . . . well, Navajos don't smoke peacepipes . . . it's not a
part of their custom. Carlton insisted they smoke a pipe and
since he was the director, the chief, the big cheese . . . he told
those Navajos that they better smoke a peacepipe or they
couldn't be released.

So, the day came to sign the treaty . . . Carlton sent a rider
clear to Oklahoma for a genuine Indian peacepipe. It took a
hundred dollars of government appropriated funds to get the pipe.
Well, the rider came back. Carlton invited the press,
government agents, and anyone else of import. So they all
gathered together. The great Manuelito, Barboncito, and Ganado
Mucho sat on the left and right side of the General. Manuelito
reluctantly lit the pipe and blew it in the four directions.
Then, he passed the pipe to the General. The General paused for
a few moments, took the pipe, held it for a few moments before he
pulled his handkerchief out of his pocket and wiped the tip of
the pipe clean . . . about twice he did this . . . he took a couple of

weak puffs and passed it on to Barboncito. Well . . . Barboncito took the pipe, held it for a few moments and while giving a cold stare to the General, he pulled out his knife . . . another dramatic moment passed and Barboncito cut the tip of the pipe off.

There was an uproar from the delegation. Carlton was so angry he started yelling at the top of his lungs for the Navajos to go home . . . to get out of there.

The Navajos looked at him and said: "— That's what we wanted to do in the first place . . . you crazy white man —."

Dirty Laundry

by Geri Keams

The Latino woman smiling, feeling at home
Her native tongue comes easily to her
There is a twinkle in her eyes as she bends
to drop the coins into the super jumbo washing machine.
They come from all over.
Looking for dreams to come true in the land
of Mickey Mouse.
The woman tells me she believes Reagan is a good man.
She don't know . . . she don't know.

There is a black man in a yellow shirt waiting for
his uniforms to dry.
He plays lonesome blues music on his harmonica
Feet tapping to the rhythm inside his heart
Black working man praising the Lord and can't
figure on the bag the government's in.
He don't know . . . he just don't know.

The Navajo Indian woman — city indian been doin'
her laundry here for 15 years.
Languages sound foreign to her . . . but full of earth.
Smiles are real to her.
They have the looks of dreamers.
Reaching out to hope . . . to chance.
Asians from Japan, Korea, the Philippines.
A young Salvadorean bangs a machine, out of order.

Navajo Indian woman thinks of talk she heard
in boarding school about the Melting Pot.
Better learn English and join the Melting Pot.
What is a Melting Pot?
The Indian wonders as she changes a dollar bill for
the dryer.
Why are all those white people moving out to the
valley for?
Don't they want to be part of the Melting Pot?

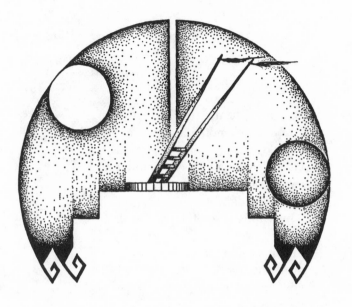

For My Hopi Friends — Shungapavi

by Geri Keams

Hopi — Second mesa
brown earth
the desert dance
of sacred song
of sacred well-rehearsed dance.
Creating rhythms
finding that certain beat
that sound
that feeling
with the womb of the earth.
It is calling out spirits of rain
in the late afternoon

lazy, hazy, heat.
There comes motion out of the ground
from kivas deep within.
Hands shaking yellow painted gourds
feet stomping earth.
Fierce winds blow
whirlwinds echo off canyon walls.

Kachina calling rain
over mad winds
with ancient music
the earth knows so well.
They dance for days
I have seen clouds dance together.
The rain spirits
falling, fast, free
wetting tongues of old warriors
deep roots, tired souls.
Rain is new strength.
Rain is new life
locusts buzz in agreement
flies go into silence
lizards come from their holes
to watch kachina — rain dancer.
They make their final exit
into red, orange, flaming sunset
zigzag up the mesa
slowly, carefully, humbled,
they walk
brownskin soaked among many colored feathers.
The song has ended.
The rain has come
as kachina climbs down the ladder into kivas
where deep within the womb
it all began many worlds ago.

Recuerdo

by Maurice Kenny

One . . . Crossings

A prune.
Humped in the front seat.
Passenger.
To July Highways,
hot winds
blowing.

A Yuma Dairy Queen
revived life
even
in the noon sun.

Two . . . Pima

rain by magic
. . .
rain by song
. . .
rain by colors
. . .
rain by dance
mountain moves
gives space to clouds
rain by magic
. . .
rain by song

Three . . . Tucson

1.
What I remember are the opals
spilling from the hide bag . . .
a deer-skin medicine bundle . . .
onto dark mahogany . . .
one rolling into a stain
of the grained wood
by a beer mug.

I remember the pistol
he took from the holster
strapped to his chest
Gently placed on the wood.

I remember my fear
running hot down my belly
running cold across my cheek.

Electricity crackled night
without a cloud in the sky . . .
in fact, the sky glittered
stars hanging low
over the sprawled city.

He chose one perfect opal
blue and pure,
placed it in my palm.
He picked up the gun . . .
    which surprised no one at all . . .
strode toward the door, swirled
around and eyed me
in a cavalry glare . . .
"I'll see you in L.A."

2.
What I remember most clearly,
vividly than any other
impression is the phone call:

Careening out   the In'dun bar
with his friend.
Both a little drunk.
The car drove aside the curb.
Seven. Young. White. Boys.
Blaaaaaaaaaaaaaaaast.
Manny and his friend.
Crumbled into their blood.

I'll sing this Papago song:

        pollen for your eyes
        tobacco for your journey
        for your eyes pollen
        for a good journey tobacco

The Arizona moonlight
now
falls into emptiness.

3.
Another memory. Sherds.
Broken on the desert.
Ancient as the mountains
rising from the floor
of the earth outside the city.

Gathered in a grass basket.
Kept safe from tourists
who would desecrate meaning
as they have desecrated
petrified wood,
paint of the desert,
kachina,
voice of Geronimo,
mountain moon,
old blood and old rain.
Sherds. Painted in thunder and wolf.

38

4.

To the woodlands man . . . humidity.
To the woodsman . . .rain
spring colors of cactus blooms.
The first Navajo taco.
First chimichanga
in the pink adobe restaurant
as he sat across the lunch table
telling us his wife
was an opera singer in Mexico City.

Cries of Apaches.
Navajos hunted like dogs
in the canyons.
Carson's laughter . . . echoes
forever, reverberates in the winds.

5.
Though I have never seen them
I remember
her horses
pounding the twilight.

I've read her letters
over and over
so perhaps I have seen
her horses.

6.
Lastly, the night
in an Oakland bar
the young Pima
told me of his country . . .
"its beauties, its beauties."
Oh, the mystery.

I watched him ride off
on his motorcycle
remembering only the beauty
mystery.
Hair streaming
long and black in the windy wake.

Four . . . Old Coyote

he sings
high
on mountain
he sings

i listen
learn
of centuries

he sings
moon
he sings
dawn follows
follows

once more

he sings
    sings

A Mohawk traveled through.

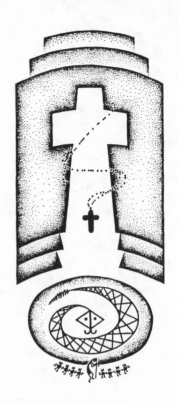

Morning Insanity

by Lomawywesa / Michael Kabotie

Yellow-red pastel horizon
quietness an ultra-marine blue
        and
thoughts, images, myths
ticker-taped among webs
along the bedroom ceiling
        Palulukung, Kukulkung, Quetzelcoatle
            the serpent peace prophets
            of the Native American
                psyche
            massacred by Christian
            paranoia and dogma

Progress, Patriotism, Profit
    rediscovered warcries
    of the techno-yuppie
      greed
    measured in Swiss Accounts
    exploited in Third World labors
    and the
    slaughter of Nature for
      pleasure and comfort

Buddha, Ghandi, Hopi
    adventurers in the humble
    and simplicity of
      life
    struggling in an adrenal
    world of terrorism, star wars
    to glimpse moments of peace
    harmony and happiness

Now

I must wake-up from my
bedroom debates and
face the cruel reality
    of an
    insane world.

Soylung Dream*

by Lomawywesa / Michael Kabotie

Cold winter
nature awaiting
to be awakened
    short days
    long nights
    snowflakes reflected
    in clear stars

In Kivas +
life being
    renewed
    blessed
    for our journey
    to forever

---

*Winter Solstice
+ Underground religious chambers

Masaui, Spirit of Birth,
Life and Death, visited
me in deep sleep

Newborn naked
crust with earth
awakened me
       I didn't recognize
       Masaui in my stupor
    With a touch
    of Birth and Death
    put me in deep sleep

On awakening
Life greeted me
with clear smiles
       told me to
       prepare my Death
              well.

I Flew Into Denver April

by Adrian C. Louis

I flew into Denver April
where salt peppered the asphalt
reflecting myself on a downtown street
where I'd paused on my route to smell lilacs.
The wanton winds chortled wickedly
over remnant snows in gray clumps of doom
and my heart soared gladly at winter's death
but an hour later I had whiskey breath
at a deadend bar packed with my race.
An Oraibi woman waltzed with me
and told me how handsome I truly was
so I bought her drinks and felt her hips
and somewhere between the grinds
and dips she lifted my wallet and split.

Shopping At Metro Mall

by Adrian C. Louis

I

Romantics will not allow the darkness
to have an unwashed smell but it does
even in the arid sterility of this city
of sand and glass where the Indian
has been relegated to artificer of artifacts,
a strange encumbrance often scorned.

Driving to Metro Mall at dusk
brief whispers of half-breed childhood
rise in the rosé sunset
In history reduced to cartoon brevity
I zig-zagged through star-shy snow
in catalog shoes bought too big,
dragging a sage branch behind.
No one would follow my tracks to the half-moon door
but halfway there I was shown my shame
by a brown gelding work horse spewing
white breath flecked with blood.
I screamed and leaped to its back
with the false lance of intellect I slashed
the darkness, Jesus,
the darkness, Jesus,
of the sky and my Indian blood.

II

With eyes of dead fish
bloated on their dreams of a white Christmas
desert peasants in polyester scourge the Mall
enforcing the sordid joy of the season.
Only the staunchest Christian
could envision Christmas in Phoenix
but I force my self to shop
because of the little girl in you,

the child who invited me down for a week in the sun.
I still view you as the pig-tailed kid
who existed before you prostrated yourself
before an alabastered Christ
and lived in a convent until your hair grayed.

The glaring and blaring Christmas shoppers
soon slip my mind past our reservation birth.
In the biggest bookstore I buy Webster's
Collegiate Dictionary because you are still
taking classes across town.
It's a good stocking stuffer I think
and stand in the checkout line wondering
and amazed that its mass should equal
Daniel Webster's.

I pay for the dictionary and exit the store.
Pretending to window shop nearby, I wait
for the blue-clad airfags.
For the first time in many years
my fists are itching and in a minute I control
the warrior craziness and breathe deeply and look
for an exit. "Silent Night" is playing
on hidden speakers
and I know tonight I will drink.

                    for Colleen

Old Lady

by Tyra Nakai

Old lady from the hogan
Getting an early rise
To take her sheep out
To graze in the mountain pastures
Bringing them in late

A Black Petal —
Amerindian Pre-history Exhibit —
Arizona, 1982

by Ralph Salisbury

Stone knife lodged
in young woman's skull — "A mystery
what brave would strike
to bone-shielded brain . ."
few fools where even cactus must choose,
from rock-miles,
where roots can thrust.

Survivor of 30 years,
my wife says maybe only
his victim's fear-
loathing-and-hate-
contorted brow not covered by his —
centuries-ravished — form,
about to be slain, he took her
with him the only way he could;

and, reading "Fighters of the time
would have prized a carefully-
shaped" — from the enormous
reaches of black strata — "blade"
sharer of six good years, I choose
to believe those loving — unable to bear
relinquished "the spoils
of battle" — this glistening black
petal — to bloom,
to this day, within a doomed brain.

Montezuma's Castle — Cliff Dwelling — Arizona

by Ralph Salisbury

("Sovapu": hole in the earth, from which
   people first issued into being — myth
              of the Hopi and others.)

For their "population explosion" —
                            when
Marco Polo was sailing
                    further from an
Historian's pen
                  than any Chinese of the day
Could have known —
                      the Sinagua built high-rise apartments,
Whole trees propped
                    big end up
                                "to support more weight" —
"Invasion" then,
                  horizon dust sighted from sentinel loft —
Or "Drought,"
                  only sand flowing through irrigation-gates,
Yearning lovers leaving
                    those "too —
Many-mouths-to-feed"
                    to shrivel in the womb.
It all disappeared
                    into scientific guesses
I read,
        a Mixed-Breed,
Surrounded by sovapu-deep
                        missile-silo tunnels.

Who Are We?

by Gabriella Sanchez

We owned the land long ago —
    Hopi
        Pima
            Navajo
In those days our life was free —
    Pueblo
        Zuni
            Cherokee
Our culture makes us proud to be —
    Papago
        Iroquois
            Apache
Our traditions will not die —
    Maricopa
    Kiva
            Yavapai
Hohokam, Yaqui, and Sioux

    Indians —
        Just to name
        a few.

Fearing Extinction

by R.T. Smith

The Anasazi potter who cindered
this stark shard's concave side
with a tribal design

must have sensed the chants turning sour,
must have known
to hide his craft inside the vessel, yet no
totem, no fetish,

no vigil in the kiva
sufficed. The whole cliff-dwelling nation
vanished forever.
                    We have the ruins,
a mound of plain
clay pots, rude glyphs in rock,
sorrow for a culture's loss
and the astronomer's promise

that *any* dying star cools
on the surface,
while within, all substance
tightens and burns,
tightens and burns.

Heraclitus Called

by R.T. Smith

religion an illness, but a noble
one, though I have had my trouble finding
spirit raised by much ritual. Still,
scavenging like a magpie for any
irregular bit of silver, I scour
the bleached tufa of Tsankawi Ruins, as yet

unexcavated and barely disturbed
by snapshooting tourists. Sun down, rangers
gone, I violate the regulations and linger,
scraping my knees on hardpan, drilling my eyes
into petroglyphs. Chambers cut
in the cliffs still harbor the deities
of the Anasazi that farmed here,
and smoke smudge shadows the crumbling ceilings,
but something more persists. Not

the spirit of the kivas forever
stalled on the ladder's aspen rungs,
clinging in patience to the upper world and lower,
not even the devout discretion of narrow paths
that would not roll a rock for convenience
into the canyon. A dance
lies implicit, its steps for corn, rain
or plentiful game still trembling the mesa,
if only slightly. Cholla

blossoms and a lazuli bunting thrums,
followed by silence wending
in and out of pinon limbs, sage, buffalo grass
and stiff vetch. I cannot move,
so certain that something hovers

larger than fact and classification, greater
even than the oblate and hammered
moon above and glowing. Slowly
I trail an instinct, a vibration changing
my blood's cadence, and the skeptic insect

in me wants to dismiss all mumbo-jumbo, insist
on the secular delight of high ground,
a horizon stained red as thimbleberry paste
and the moon jewel soaring free
of clouds, but then the wind drives me
to all fours, dust stinging,
and the great song of air scolding between
the sandstone channels approaches hymn.
Downcast, I find two bits

of some practical neolithic bowl
with fragments, of the rain serpent perhaps, preserved,
and one begins to shift
position, miraculous in itself until I see
the carpenter ant beneath, another delver who
dismisses what impedes him or
what he cannot quite disbelieve in. So this

is the moment. I accept the gift and catch
cholla's near invisible needles in my hand
for pain's proof that real is real. Down
then I climb, into the cool kiva's clay scent, its cloy,

and feel dark fill it with stillness. Not
ghosts of mere memory, but something half-tangible and unafraid.
Half an hour, and I am again
aloft and seeking the aura of some workless thing

I suspect I've divined, but
no luck, the same atmosphere can't be twice
touched, as nocturnal creatures stir

and I descend slowly, thankful for every rung, limb
and ledge, as I feel now somehow brother
to the woodtick riding a muledeer's muscle,
to the skunk's pungent must
and the gall wasp's flutter where wind
unsettles the spare larch needles. Nearby coyotes

pick up the indefinite message
of this place. A sidewinder scrawls his own brief
glyph in sand, as I hold up one shard
to the moonlight's shimmer and admit
to mystery's invitation, cholla splinters in my palm,
the lure and more, the desert promise
of an indistinct ailment
I have spent half a life in flight form. Is it subtle

and at once conspicuous? It is
bitter, transfiguring, flaming and sweet.

Mirage

by R.T. Smith

So one day in frustration
at the unnamables, forsaking the cottonwoods,
avocados and radio salsa, I walked out,
first down chaparral with its wrung
judas trees and sage, past pinon, grama grass
and cholla, carried only water, a hat
with full visor and the compass. North I went

toward a blue and distant
mountain impossibly steep. The sun's
persistence and absence of shadows. The needle's
steady tremble. My dance. I struck
a basin with wind so steady that sand rose
membranous, and not even my own tracks
would follow. This was exact:
the land of scorpion, sidewinder, heat and deception:
the threats we can name no
matter how hard the inner

wilderness insists, no matter how vast
white bleakness grows. O'Keefe could have rendered it
safe and abstract, a beauty glowing
for necessary form, but I stumbled, grew angry, saw
the sun begin descent and started back, against
the arrow's red tip,
south toward water's sweet coil about
every riverstone. Stunned

by dune-shift and the swirlstorms
of sharp dirt, I wandered
degrees from my azimuth across the silver basin
of hammered haze, anarchy of the elements. Yes,

I was thirsty, lonely, unfriendly to every
motion that might attack, anything
insistent enough to be not-me, but

cresting a ridge I saw it,
a disturbance as the mountain
turned around, disassembled,
became a flock of sweet pinon jays dazzled by some
force in the sand. A cluster,
a series of forms implying one
icon, they whorled blue and indigenous,
sure they belonged. Clouds
blossomed to orchards of bone. Ripe for drama,
I dropped to my knees and felt the thin tears evaporate,

then rose, somehow healed or filled
with the requisite illusion of destination
or cure to carry this
vision of small birds
swarming over an anthill back southward
into alpine woods and lush-rooted gardens, into
civilization, its wry taxonomies, certain
I could carry it to my grave
as a comfort, a passport,
and leave it here as well
in drifting words.

Coyotes' Desert Lament

by Mary Tallmountain

I lie on the little hill
Reading a scroll of stars
Moon soars, staring.
My hound stirs restless.
On the far mesa a coyote yaps.

Hound steel still
Dark, wolfish shadow.
Does he remember ancient fires,
Peaceful before he heard
The long howl of his brothers?

From the river willows
Two coyotes reply.
Scissors of sound slice mist.
Across the valley
Drops a silent waiting.

Suddenly I am coyote too,
Nose a wet black tremble.
Hound and I bunch together
Among warm grey bodies
Calling our brother home.

Phoenix Night-Watch

by Mary Tallmountain

Growling and muttering,
a jet shoulders down
into the Valley of the Sun.
I remember running to watch
the 1936 mail-plane after dark,
its flashing red/green eyes.

From the country road
smells of gasoline and melted tar
drift with oleander spice
across drenched grass.
Lingering heat arouses sleeping
pheromones of scent.

Betelgeuse peers down
through orange dustclouds.
Baby gecko quivers on my toe,
thinking it's a twig,
I sit so still,
waiting.

I think you'll come again
tonight, Hohokam Indian man,
to guard your hidden treasure —
a net of finely wrought canals
buried in red earth
sifted out of little mountains.

Guard, my ancient brother,
your worthy works.
Your bones lie folded
through this millennium
in the land you left to us
unscarred.

We watch, sleeping Indian,
woman, reptile,
earth and planet —
in mysterious fusion
with desert night.

Summer Storm

by Phyllis Wolf

It is always very late
before the sun completely dies
in summer. The colors are first
furious but then resign themselves
peacefully. This sun seems
to fight much more furiously
this evening, reddening the entire
sky. I watch it sing behind
the furrows of bottomland
I lay in. The ridges are dark
and deep but not deep enough
for the wind that ripples my skirt.
My husband's shoulders
became round his first year.
Round like the shoulders of other
men who work the fields. I would
watch him gather stones
smaller than the center of my palm
from fields. He would drop
them into a canvas sack
and drag the sack to a corner
of a forty. He wanted nothing
to hinder shoots of wheat
that would soon come from black
soil. The air, heavy in untended
June blossoms and newly toiled earth,
is heavier still this evening.
Nothing moves but the sky
that lights the east and south.
The heaviness of the air
has made the field sweat.
It sticks to my arm.
Bolts rip a dark sky miles away.
It will be only a few hours before
the winds come. My husband never
saw a fierce summer storm

and watched bolts break and race
across the sky. The thunderbolt
struck clean. Minutes passed
before the hole began to bleed.
The skin was seared blacker than
furrowed bottomland. He didn't
seem surprised but still
wondrous of a sky that would bring
life to the stillness that lay
in black fields.

Our Dog's Life

by Mike Medicine Horse Zillioux

Kerosene stained dandruff.
Wish we had a shower or water. Running.
Smokey sleeping on a torn couch. Dog,
Dreaming of clods and tails.

Wood ticks in the summer,
Manes like lions with no hair. Bald.

Wash basins and tin pans.
A spider in the bathing tub.

Used up match books,
Tamarisks which won't bend.

Ink and pencil markings on the wall.
The children remembered that from school.
Boarding and day schools.

No English and no biting of nails.
Bow ties and weekly haircuts.

On the chin and the jaw and don't forget the ears.

Dogs are only old woman talking before the visitors arrive.

Too often tossed out of a whiteman's car.

1976

A Single Woman

by Mike Medicine Horse Zillioux

Eliza was the only child left in the village.
She was always aware of the shadows, echoes and stares
Of the old ones. Finally,
They called her wild spinach.
For the way she always asked to go.
For years, they watched her come to the banks
And bend and cut the plant.

They hid her from the government agent.
He took the others to Oklahoma and Kansas.
Put into railcars and shipped to schools.

She learned the old ways.
She listened to animals.
And soon she changed her name to Grayeyes.
The color never changed and remained as empty.
And clear as the clouds of rain.

And she became a woman.
Tall and dark with the tatoo pulling her mouth.
A laughing smile and touching hands,
That called the men to her.

She had been known to make men fall into her bed,
Pulling pubic hair as they slept. Grayeyes was feared and abused.
She was cast as an odd one.
A woman who had caused her neighbors crops to fail,
In an otherwise plentiful year.

She grew in her strength to make men come to her house.
To make them cry.
As animals.

For this Grayeyes watched the other women laugh,
Fortune was their husbands and sons.
Coming to her. Blackening their faces.

Fearing something more than the Apaches.
More than hunger.
More than being alone.

1988

Essays

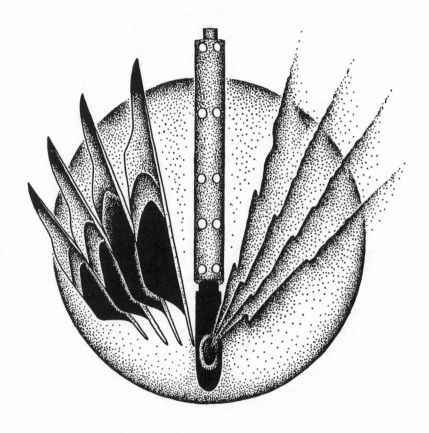

 *My Uncle Sam — The Storyteller*

by Barbara A. Antone

A long, long time ago, storytelling was a favorite past time for Yuman Indian families. It was a source of fun and entertainment after a long hard day of work. The family would sit under a cluster of sparkling, glittery stars on a clear summer night, eating watermelon waiting for the storyteller to begin. Each family had its own storytellers. Our family storyteller was Uncle Sam, a man in his early 70's with shoulder length pepper-gray hair, a prickly stubbed beard and bushy moustache to match. Crows feet would appear along the side of his eyes when he laughed. As I remember, Sam lived a long life full of mischievous adventures. Before beginning a story, he always chuckled to himself. Sam loved to tell Coyote stories. Coyote was his favorite character and he portrayed him as sly, wicked, and mischievous. He was always an old man. I used to think that he sometimes thought of himself playing the role of the Old Coyote.

Although I listened to the stories, I hardly understood them. Being seven years of age, I had to use my own childish imagination. I thought that the funny noises he made with his voice and the facial expressions he used were funny. I later learned that the coyote stories were told for adults. Younger children could not understand them because they were not yet mature, and they weren't able to understand the moral behind the stories.

As I grew older and heard repeated coyote stories, I too, started to burst out laughing, just like the elder members of my family did when Uncle Sam concluded his stories.

The coyote stories, to me, portrayed a fun-loving individual who enjoyed a carefree life and never gave thought to the serious aspect of everyday living. He was hilarious, comical, and in a sense, loveable. Most of the stories were told about a husband-wife relationship. For example, the story below:

Coyote Gets Married

Fun-loving, lazy, Old Coyote who never worked or hunted for food, almost in his entire life, finally found himself a lady and got married. One day, Old Coyote asked his wife to cook him a pot of beef stew. Without giving a thought of putting meat on the table, he left the house for a long leisurely stroll. This wasn't the first time he did this. The wife got tired of his lazy bad habits and decided to put a stop to his laziness. She found his old beat up leather shoes and decided to cook it in the stewpot. After a long walk, Old Coyote thought of the home-cooked beef stew and got hungry. He rushed home to eat. When he got home, he got the surprise of his lifetime. His wife was cooking his old leather shoes. He got very angry. He asked his wife in an angry tone, "Why are you cooking my shoes?!" The wife replied, "Let this be a lesson to you, Old Coyote, if you can't provide meat for our table, then you deserve to eat your old shoes."

MORAL: A lazy worthless man who spends the rest of his entire life in leisure will soon come to the end of his road.

Each storyteller shares a family story. Although the dates, times, and places differ, each story remains similar in essence. The storytellers have their own unique way of sharing. Storytellers have a natural talent in teaching philosophy. Uncle Sam died around age 80 and before he died, he carved out of a silverspoon, three heart-shaped rings and gave them to us. Sam is remembered through his storytelling talents. He left for us an important teaching tool to use in educating our children in philosophy. It is a tradition we must carry on for our future generation as well.

Black Mesa Blues
by Dan L. Crank

Once, Navajos had old legends about evil giants roaming the land. Like modern television heroes, Navajo twin heroes exterminated the beasts at hand. Today, these reincarnated giants are back, chewing and disemboweling the sand and soil of the Black Mesa. First, the Navajo family is told to move to a new site. Next, the century-old junipers and sages are cleared. In the next series of destructions, layers of earth are ripped out with explosives and machinery. Like a butchered cow, the land exposes her vital organs. If the Company butcher does not find quality, black elements, then the hole is filled back up in haste. But the damage is irreversible. They reclaim only the top layer of sand. They do not even apologize to the startled and shocked animals on the land.

Before the Metal Giants came, the Black Mesa valleys were fertile and heavily wooded. In brown, gray soil, junipers, shrub oaks and wildflowers stood or leaned in the slight cool breeze. Sheep, cattle, and wild animals had their natural territories. On early spring mornings, tracks of night animals wove in and out of bushes, arroyos, and burrows. Clear snow water trickled down from the forests' shades to dozens of arroyos, where puddles formed in corners, and animals sipped at these, at their pleasure. In time, the puddles in the corners overflowed, then the water ran to the next pool. At the end, the chain of puddles created a little stream which a lucky Navajo farmer might use to start his spring crops. Once, before the Metal Giants, before the first surveyor's red ribbons, all was quiet, peaceful, and friendly.

A decade ago, on assignment to locate a Navajo student, I drove from Kayenta to the top of Black Mesa. I took the dirt mine road down a steep hill and through a deep arroyo. At the top of the arroyo was a small coal mining operation. It seemed not so threatening and was well hidden from view in the heavy, tall woods. I drove through areas that had dense forest of junipers and pinons. A pencil-drawn map helped me; otherwise, I would have been lost. Beyond one rusted, crimson windmill, the road led into bushy hills, then another windmill appeared. This one was painted silver. The trough held greenish water. Further ahead, through a clearing in the forest, I saw a hogan, a large lumber house, and other dwellings in a sloped valley. Before all that was an arroyo, which had a thin stream when I drove across it. In spring, snowmelt probably raged through here. Besides the arroyo was a small cornfield. An ageless scarecrow peacefully guarded its home. It was a lost, beautiful valley. I remember well the rough, rutted road, but the view made it worthwhile.

At the hogan, an old Navajo grandmother, a young Navajo mother with a child, and a teenage girl greeted me. They knew I would come, even though I was days late. Word was sent beforehand about someone coming to pick up the teenage student. The women said the roads had been bad, and they thought I had been swallowed by the mire some place, or else, I had not even attempted to drive their road. In the large house made of cement blocks and lumber, we talked over hot coffee. I was a stranger but they received me like a fellow clan member. The house was smoothed over with gray mortar, stucco-style. In the distance, white spots of sheep and goats grazed. Bells or cries of birds lingered in the background of our conversation.

At last the Navajo girl was ready, and we loaded her stuff into the truck. Chickens flapped their wings at the ashpile, as we left. The girl's grandmother had made bread and mutton sandwiches. We would get soda pop along the way, back on the main highway. The teenager told me that she had missed school for two weeks because she couldn't get a ride back; the mud made it impossible. She said, just watch though, someone would be coming in with supplies today for her grandmother. Every way one looked, it was woods, hills, bushes, and clear blue sky. Sure enough, halfway out of another valley, we saw clouds of dust rising from the woods. Soon, a four wheel drive truck zoomed towards us, and then with a slight swerve, it passed. Someone waved. The girl quietly said that that was the truck but it was alright; grandma would tell them she left.

A couple of years later, the mass destruction was widespread. The beautiful valleys of Black Mesa were going to shreds. Machinery, drag-lines, dump trucks, oil and grease stains, bull-dozed trees, coal dust, carved hills and "contaminated water" signs were everywhere. Some-where along the line, the destruction reached that valley I visited years back. Firewood gatherers, like vultures onto a major kill, followed the clearing sites. Useable and crushed wood were easy to gather and load. I had driven on a nice leveled road over a wooded hill. Around the bend, at the next clearing, I came upon a homesite. Suddenly, it all came back to me; this was the place, the lost valley in the middle of nowhere. Now, it probably had a name or a number because of the mining and the sur-veying. The dwellings were the same — hogan, large house, water bar-rels and woodpile — but somehow it felt too exposed. A Navajo woman in faded clothing stood by the house and peered at the heavy dust created by two trucks before me. Maybe she was cursing us. The fine road dust appeared to have settled on everything. The gray appearance gave it a strange and sad feeling.

A year later, only the large house stood. Nearby, temporary homes, trailers and campers had been positioned under juniper trees at the edge of the valley clearing. The miners had moved in to be closer to their jobs. Already their carelessness showed. Metal cans, glass and trash sites scarred the valley.

The next summer, someone appeared to still live in the house, and the cornfield seemed to still be used. The sad peaceful scarecrow was gone. A couple of rag flags flapped on the tallest poles at the edge of the field. A lone figure of a woman, perhaps that of the young mother, stood in the middle of the field. I thought of stopping and asking her questions but the damage was already done. I would be an outsider, and I would probably startle her. She ignored the mine trucks and woodgatherers that traveled near her home and cornfield. Her figure seemed to suggest that the matter was over with; they had resisted and lost. This would be her last crop; then she would move away like the others had done.

Last winter, I drove on the smooth, wide, tar-drenched road to near the once beautiful valley to gather dry juniper fire-wood. This time around, the house was gone. A few boards and broken foundations were exposed in the warm winter sun. I drove in silence through the valley, across the dry, empty arroyo, past the weedy cornfield, and past oily trash scattered all the way to the other side of the valley. It appeared that this was no longer regarded as a homesite; the final exodus had been made. They left behind a broken, chewed valley. Now, only tumbleweeds embedded with mine dust rolled alongside the dusty and filthy mine roads.

The Metal Giants are still gnawing and spitting out the soil and vegetations of Black Mesa. They have ruined the water tables. Now, it's unsafe for man or animal to drink from the arroyo springs. In a decade, the happiness of a Navajo family, the lushness of a peaceful valley, and the integrity of a Mesa have been destroyed.

Fountain of the Kachinas

by Valerie Jackson

The early morning breeze carries with it a cool freshness, which complements the soothing sounds of falling water. Doves bathe in a reservoir of water that collects beneath the feet of the guardians of the fountain — the Kachinas. Facing the west is Eototo, the Chief of the Kachinas, who is only one of the many Water Spirits of the Pueblo peoples inhabiting the Southwest. Eototo, about four feet high, is carved of stone. His necklace is etched deep in his chest and his head is simple, with only round spaces for his eyes and mouth. His attire consists of a long blouse and skirt and his feet appear bare, but could also have moccasins. It is hard to tell because a stone carving is not as finely detailed as a wooden carving. To the north and south of Eototo are the profiles of two fellow spirits: Chakwaina, a common dancer, and Hano Mana, a Tewa Kachina.

The Kachina facing east is not visible, but he is the one who greets the sun with his square head and large ears first; he is called a common Kachina.

The people pray to the Kachina Spirits to bring rain to their sun-parched lands. Survival depends upon delicate balances between Father Sun, Mother Earth and the various Water Spirits. Kachinas, in a physical sense, are either human, dressed in their colorful, elaborate costumes, or they are intricately carved from the root of the cottonwood tree, with attention paid to every minute detail; here Eototo and his companions are carved of stone.

The four Kachinas comprise the pedestal that supports the bowl-shaped reservoir above their heads. This, in turn, contains an 18-inch pedestal that supports a smaller bowl from which the fountain erupts. As the stream flows down over the lip of the larger bowl, droplets of water converge in a continual sheet that gently flows down onto Eototo and his Water Spirit companions. The sun has recently risen, yet the fountain remains in shadow, because the rays of sunlight have not yet crested the roof of the red brick building to the east. Despite the shade, Eototo and his companions celebrate the entrance of Father Sun and the new day by observing the morning bathing ritual of the doves at their feet. Some of the birds are perched on cornerstones which have symbols on them that are representations of the clouds, the carriers of the life-giving rains so crucial to the survival of Mother Earth and her inhabitants.

A fountain is an ironic place for the Kachina Water Spirits to be. It is as though the peoples' prayers for rain are being answered continually, not feeding the dry earth, but by filling the reservoirs of the fountain where birds bathe and students come to soothe their weary minds and be refreshed by the sounds of the burbling water. Ancient Eototo and his companions seem to be out of place and time surrounded by enormous buildings on a modern university campus. But, the Kachinas also seem to be right at home, as the guardians on the pedestal of the fountain and at the center of the Pueblo peoples' existence.

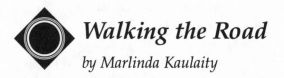 *Walking the Road*

by Marlinda Kaulaity

This telling was inspired by my nephew whose first steps brought scattered images together into one. . . .

I

The night was cloudless and the stars glittered distinctly in the blackness of the clear sky. The moon filled the flat countryside with its silver glow. All the land around was serene and silent, except for the hushed sounds coming from activity inside the tipi. The tipi by the old stone house stood tall and spread out in a dignity all its own. Its lone eagle feather waved gently from the highest pole; smoke passed over it and curled upward into the velvet of the stardust sky. The whole tipi was a living thing, now quiet and breathing in the pure night air. Shadows of the people inside could be seen through the slanted canvas walls.

The voice of the crackling fire was loud and its flames were high enough to make the people comfortably warm. The handle of the water bucket clanged as it hit the rim whenever a new person drank water at this midnight hour. Everyone sat silently during this break from their spiritual communication. Sitting cross-legged on his padded cushion east of the fire, the firekeeper looked around at the other people in the tipi, and he seemed satisfied that his prayer had reached the Creator.

"This represents the road of life," Grandpa said gently as he gestured to the crescent sand moon lying spread out in front of him.

"A human being starts out as a little baby — crawling, needing other's care, having no teeth, until the first few cut through. It's a very special time."

The people listened attentively as the water was still being passed around the tipi clockwise. I drank some cool mountain water and blessed myself with its life. Farther around the circle, sleepy children awoke to take a drink. A few men, out of their kneeling positions, found ways to quietly stretch their legs while waiting for the water. Women fixed loose hair and very discreetly stretched their legs too. Some elderly people wiggled side to side to relieve their backs and to prepare for the oncoming morning.

"When you get to the center here," he pointed to the place where the Chief sat, "you're halfway through your life, probably about 50 years old." He shifted the weight of his body to get comfortable and leaned forward a little. Around his neck hung his old red and blue blanket, and he sat dignified and strong as he spoke.

"Then when you get near the end of the road over there," he pointed toward the tapered sand at the northeast end of the moon, "you start looking like you did when you first started out. You don't have very many teeth left; you need your younger relations to help you get around; and you have trouble walking and balancing yourself like a little baby just learning to walk does. You may even have to crawl again."

. . . . I thought then of Dad's old grandma who toward the very end of her life used to crawl on the earth floor of the hogan. Her hair was white as the many winters she had seen in her lifetime, and her wrinkles were like the land, worn deep from nature's timeless hand. She kept the hogan door open and enjoyed sitting on the earth, letting the sun's rays touch her now dormant eyes. She greeted us with a soft handshake, a gentle touching of palms, enough for us to feel each other's being. Then she spoke about events in her day that made us laugh and feel closely bound to one another. Her words, laughter, and gestures told me that even in her old age, she still had a wonder, respect, and awe of life's everyday mysteries.

The relatives in the tipis's circle sat gazing into the fire perhaps lost in their own memories. Grandpa had spoken and we had reflected upon his words and this life. That night we all listened, remembered, and learned from Grandpa, whose wisdom was respected by many. The midnight water ceremony passed and the morning star came quickly, bringing after it early dawn's yellow-orange rays. They spread across the horizon like a woven rug dyed with plants carefully picked.

II

The day I went to the PHS hospital was a typical Fort Defiance day — sunny and bright. No breeze moved the air, just warm sun on brown skin. People of all ages were coming and going through the hospital's wide double doors. A young Navajo couple came out together, obviously anxious to get home. The woman carried a bulging plastic bag of belongings; the man held a tiny bundle of pink softness in his big arms. He looked from beneath his large cowboy hat at his new daughter as his wife walked a few steps behind him. Love and pride colored his face. In a government van parked by the emergency entrance, an old man sat in the back seat staring at nothing, waiting for nothing. Such variation in life's cycles were alive on this particular day. A family of five, spirited and restless, stood on the sidewalk waiting to get a quick lunch. Others sat outside at tables set there especially for eating out on days like this.

As I neared the snack bar, I could smell hamburgers sizzling on the grill inside. My stomach groaned at the smell of food and I felt a bit hungry, but I had an appointment. That fact shouldn't have hurried me as it did because even with an appointment, there is seemingly endless waiting at PHS. Tiny little babies, old people, and all others in between fill the waiting rooms everyday to wait and wait as if nothing else mattered except hearing their names called. Their illnesses almost seem unimportant, as if just hearing the sound and rhythm of their names was their sole purpose for being there. They wait.

Just as I got to the cement steps nearer to the hospital, I looked over to the left where an old Navajo woman sat cozily in the grass against an old oak tree. She sat in a reverent kind of way — kneeling on the earth and feeling the gentleness of the day. She was dressed in the traditional long skirt and velveteen blouse. Her flowered scarf was pulled over her white hair a little past her forehead, shading the bright sun from her eyes. She wore round wire-rimmed glasses and red tennis shoes. I, too, thought her spot was a much nicer place to wait, better than sitting inside the hospital with the sickness, pain, and fear.

When it was time for her to leave she began shifting her body out of its relaxed position. She leaned forward very slowly, placing both wrinkled hands on the ground in front of her, and very carefully lifted her fragile old body. Her knees were shaking slightly in this bent-over position. A few seconds passed. Then she gradually raised the upper portion of her small body and stood with arms outstretched, like a tightrope walker above a circus crowd. She didn't move, only stood awhile trying to balance herself. She quickly glanced around to see if anyone had seen her awkwardly trying to rise and walk. Nobody but me noticed this assiduous feat.

The old woman smiled then, like she was proud of what she had just done. In a way, she seemed amused at herself, about how she had to go through such a ceremony just to get walking. Her smile revealed only a few teeth surrounded by smooth pink gums, and it brought out all the wrinkles on her face. She dusted off her skirt, adjusted her scarf, and then slowly walked across the grass to the hospital on the other side of the street.

III

"Willie's getting daring," Mary said, "he's not afraid to walk anymore." Willie was still a baby with long soft hair hanging in the back of his head and over his big black eyes. Navajo custom says not to cut a baby's hair until after he talks, and so Willie still had the baby hair he was born with. He had his first birthday just a few days before he started his quest to walk. Before his recent daring, he crawled around real fast and liked to sit under Grandma's table, the one with the center wooden leg that looked like it had toes. He laughed his baby laugh as he playfully picked on the old calico cat who just lay there ignoring him.

I sat in the living room watching Willie and his escapades under the table. My mind took me back to the time I was told about the old man who called a special song to honor all the little Indian children at the Pow-Wow. . .

"Being close to the earth is a powerful place," the old man from Denver had said. The little children dressed in their "Indian clothes" listened as they stood around the arena before *their* song. They were the center of attention. Fathers and grandfathers around the drums hit the hides hard and whooped their cries of approval. Mothers and grandmothers looked lovingly and proudly at their little ones dressed in the clothes they had woven, beaded, and decorated. Seeing their children in their finery let them know the time spent making these special clothes was very worthwhile.

The old man continued, "Only babies and small children really feel this special power because they're closest to our Mother Earth. They, too, have a kind of power and they receive the earth's secrets and use them in their own way."

. . . . My thoughts were interrupted by the cat who ran out of the kitchen into the bedroom to hide. Willie squealed and bounced up and down and I knew he had done something to make the old cat run out so fast. He crawled into the living room where we all sat, making little excited noises. He stopped awhile and sat as if pondering what to do next.

And then it happened — he decided to walk. He got on his little knees with his hands in front of him, pushed his little body forward, and then raised his diapered bottom upward. Still bent over and balancing on his tiny fingertips and strong chubby legs, he contemplated this new exploit. He kept his eyes fixed on the floor, staring at it, studying its secrets, and then he slowly raised himself up, his arms held outward. It must have looked like a long way down to Willie, but actually it was less than a foot to the floor. He just stood there awhile, eyes big with wonder, enjoying the moment. He looked around at all of us watching his moves; then he took a step forward, arms still balancing and eyes still fixed. He took another step and then another until he fell back into a sitting position onto the floor. Looking around at all our faces, he innocently smiled.

We all clapped for Willie. He realized he had done something new and different; his giggles and baby noises as he bounced himself up and down told us he liked this feeling. His big smile revealed only a few baby teeth and his whole soft face became part of the smoke. Through his black hair hanging in his face, we could see his big round eyes sparkling with delight. We were all happy for him. Willie would now begin his journey on that long road of life. . . .

Marana Cotton Fields

by Mercy Molina-Whillock

The scent of the damp earth and the wet desert plants is refreshing and soothing. Always after rainfall, I remember images of my father, walking in the distance, a shovel on his shoulder, wearing black rubber boots and a worn earth-colored felt hat set at an angle on his head. He trudges through the mud, checking the water, making sure that the cotton plants are getting their fill. He steps in the middle of the field until he finds what he's looking for. The furrows are clogged, damming the water so that it cuts across the rows, leaving a dry patch of cotton in the middle of the field.

I dig my toes in the mud, sailing little twigs in the ripples of the water, watching them swirl away down the green tunnels of the cotton rows. I spot a green-hued passenger for my little green boat. He's busy, unaware of me, the conductor, contemplating sending him on a trip down the green tunnel. He curls up at my touch and digs his heels into the green carpet of his home. He's soft and dainty and I can't lift him without hurting him, so I cut his home away from its moorings and set it adrift in the ripples. It swirls around and around, a raft with a frightened curled-up passenger in the middle, clinging insistently. I watch him drift away until he disappears from view.

I peek over the cotton plants. My father's still shoveling, whistling through his teeth. He never whistles like other men, puckering their lips to make clear sharp sounds. He makes soft hissing tones, almost a whisper at times. I always wondered why he never whistled loud, but I never asked. That's just the way my father whistles.

I wiggle my toes in the mud, then decide to finish my chores. They're not really chores. I don't have to do them, but I do. It's kind of fun, learning to irrigate. I put my shoes on and skip over to start the hoses to the dry section of the field. My father showed me how to start the hoses. He used to laugh at my efforts. Now he leaves me to start the water. There's a trick to it. The hoses are almost too big for my small hand to cover one end. The other you stick in the ditch of water and by covering the top end and dipping the bottom, you create a suction. When the water gushes up you throw it down in between the cotton rows. Sometimes, when I didn't do it right, the water would gush up heavily and the six foot hose would get too hard to hold and I'd find myself wet and sitting in the mud. That's why my father would laugh. But my eight year old 'sitdown' could handle it. It didn't hurt. It was funny and fun and made my father laugh.

I see him stretching to see over the cotton. He's looking for me. I wave and let him know where I am and that I'm safe. I continue to start each hose, row by row until there are a bunch of little creeks bubbling and gurgling. The hot breeze picks up the moisture and scent; it smells and feels good. I used to like it so much, that I would dip my finger in the mud and lick it. He put a stop to that. I see him swing the shovel on his shoulder and start back up the rows. I know it's lunch time, because there is no shadow. He taught me that too. I can make a clock by sticking a stick in the ground and noting the direction of the shadow — I can tell time. I run to the truck to get the lunch that Mom made for him and that I brought to the fields. My toes can barely reach the pedals, and I have to stretch to see over the dash board, but I can drive. Sometimes when I'm driving, the other workers see me and honk their horns. Sometimes I honk back, but most of the time I'm too busy driving. He taught me to drive, because somebody had to bring his lunch. I share only a little of his lunch, because I can go home and eat, but he has to stay until the sun goes down.

Sometimes he irrigates at night, but he won't take me then. He says it's not safe, that I might fall in the water and he won't be able to see me. Besides, it's not what a little Yaqui girl should be doing. This is men's work!

Short Stories

Going Home

by Joseph Bruchac

"Look, Tommy, down there in the valley. Look at all those little houses the white people have made. Look at how they are all like little boxes, those houses in that little town of theirs. They always like to build in the valleys like those, the white people."

The new Ford van rolled along the four-lane highway as Jake Marsh pointed with one long brown finger out the window on the passenger side, the imitation "Indian" accent coming out from between lips held carefully unmoving. The half-smile of trickster was on his face, a can of ginger ale in his other hand. Behind the wheel, Tom Hill shook his head and laughed silently.

"Yes," Tom said, "yes."

"Oooh, Tommy, maybe there is a college in that town. Yes, there is a college there. Maybe it is the college where Sonny is going to school. He has been in college a long time."

"Twelve years," Tom said, coughing.

"He is always writing us for money, Tommy. He is a good boy. He is going well in the college. Some day we are going to go and see him. If he ever tells us where the college is. All of us are going to go see him."

"All of us," Tom said, "all 120 of us."

"Yes, we will go there for his graduation and have a giveaway. We will give away many blankets. Then he can come home. They say at the Agency they have a good job for him. Janitor. That will be a good job for an Indian boy. It will have vacation time."

"Retirement benefits," Tom said, trying to keep his face straight.

"Tommy, you know he has a girl there at the college. But he will not tell us about her. I think mebbe she is white."

"She's white."

"But Sonny won't have any children by her. He is going to come back home and marry Dolores Antelope. She comes from a good family, even if they are a little stupid. Yes, when he comes home he will marry Dolores. She has been waiting for him."

Only 20 years now," Tom said. Then he started laughing.

Jake Marsh laughed too. They laughed at the person Jake had been for a while, that gentle, bemused tone in the voice, that simple way of saying and seeing which — even as they laughed at it — was laughing at them, laughing with them. Jake drained the can of ginger ale and began striking his palm against the dashboard, beating out the rhythm of a 49-er:

"Someday we will be together
till eternity, ah whey ya hi ya hi . . ."

He sang it in a low voice first, then higher with each repetition. Tom strained his own vocal cords to stay with it until both of them were singing in voices thin as the last note of a coyote's call. Tom's throat felt tight and good. The song stopped and they listened for a while to the silence. Then Jake began striking the dashboard again, trying to find another beat. "Funny," he said, "when I used to drink, I could remember a thousand songs. Now it's hard to remember one." He crushed the ginger ale can and put it into the plastic litter bag hanging from the knob of the glove compartment.

The hills tolled up from the river near the road. On top of a few hills single pine trees stood. They looked like men with arms held out from their sides, waiting for something. Tom thought that for a moment, then shook his heads. No, not men, trees. The trees looked like trees. It had been a long time since he had seen them this way.

"When I was at Fort Grant," he said. Then he stopped. He had to let the words come together in the right way. Jake sat, waiting for him. Five miles passed. A red-tail hawk glided over the road, heading west. Tom took in a deep breath. "There weren't too many Indians there. Most of them were Pima or Papago, in for stealing something while they were drunk, most of them. One or two for murder — the murderers are the ones you can trust, you know. It's the ones who forge checks that are the worst. You can't trust them. But the murderers, you could always trust them. One was a guy from Oklahoma. His name was Harold Buffalo. His uncle is that painter. I met his sister in Tulsa once."

"Was her name Mary?" Jake said.

"Yes, it was. She had a little boy, too."

"Ah-hah," Tom said. He shifted his hands on the wheel and pointed with his lips at the sign which read REST AREA. Jake shook his head and they passed the turn-off without slowing down. Tom took another deep breath. "There wasn't anything in the prison for us then. It was so far out in the desert it cost wives and girlfriends more than $20 to come and visit. It was called a 'Rehabilitation Center.' For rehabilitation, ree-hah-bill-ih-tay-shun, they would have us build walls. Long stone walls. They looked like the Great Wall of China, except they were about four feet tall, the walls we built. They had us build them at the base of the mountain that rose behind the prison. That mountain was beautiful. You could feel its breath. But there was nothing for us in Fort Grant. So we asked to be allowed to have a sweat lodge. It would have to be sponsored by someone, we were told. There were sweat lodges in other prisons, but none there — even though now there were 20 of us who were Indians and we knew we needed it. Damn."

"Right rear tire," Jake said.

Tom pulled the van over to the side of the road. The flat tire went wha-that wha-that on the pavement and then growled into the gravel. Both men got out and stretched. They walked up the grassy bank and sat down. It was a crisp day in early September. The air was sweet as spring water. Jake leaned on one elbow to look closely at a small plant.

"It says I should pick it."

"Your uncle was the medicine man," Tom said. He looked at the plant. They were both smiling, but Jake pulled the small plant up and wrapped it in his handkerchief, leaving a little tobacco on the ground near the grains of gravel which came up with the roots. They walked back to the van and began to change the tire. They worked with the quick ease of men who had spent many years doing that sort of thing. When they were done they spat, wiped their hands on the seats of their jeans and got back in.

Jake sat behind the wheel. He started the engine. "What did you do next?" he said. He put the truck into gear.

"We did it their way first. We went to the prison chaplain. There was one. For all faiths — Methodist, Baptist, Catholic, Mormon, Jewish, even the Black Muslims. He was a Catholic priest from Boston, Father Milley. He was so thin we used to say he didn't dare cross his legs for fear he'd cut his knees. He told us that a sweat lodge was not possible. That was when Harold Buffalo spoke up. 'There is going to be a sweat lodge here, sir,' he said. 'When something like that is going to happen, you can't stop it.'"

"Did they interpret that as a threat. First they thought of transferring Harold. Then they remembered all the times he had asked to be transferred from Fort Grant and decided that wasn't much of a punishment, maybe even it was what he wanted them to do. Finally they decided to cut off his privileges. When they let him out of the hole, he was told he could no longer have rec with the other men. But he didn't mind. He started to run by himself every day. First he ran a mile. Then he ran two miles. By the time they decided to let him back into population, he was running ten miles every day. He had been a Green Beret and he knew a lot about survival in the desert. That worried the prison authorities because everyone in Arizona remembered The Fox."

"I heard of him in Nevada," Jake said. "Another Green Beret."

"The Fox escaped from Florence. He'd been in for killing four men — two of them police. He knew he'd never be allowed to get away, so he didn't even try to get to Mexico. He didn't try to escape any further. He just stayed out in the desert near the prison. Nights he would sneak into the camps of the men hunting him and steal their food. He even climbed back over the walls of the prison and left his calling card — right where the Captain stepped in it first thing next morning. It took them a long time to catch The Fox, but they say they finally did. Caught him in a box canyon and shot him to pieces. But none of the other inmates ever saw his body. Some say he is still out there or he finally did make it to Mexico. So the authorities kept a close eye on Harold because they remembered The Fox. But all Harold did was run, just run further and faster each day, around and around inside the prison fence."

Tom pulled out a pack of Camels and shook two loose. Jake took one and lit both cigarettes with his lighter. The lighter was covered with red and blue beads making the pattern of a thunderbird. The smoke was blue inside the cab of the blue van. The smell of the tobacco was strong. Jake nodded to the right and Tom nodded. They took the exit. There was a police car pulled over near the toll both. Tom opened the glove compartment and slid the automatic pistol out without looking at it, his eyes straight ahead. He put the gun between his legs and covered it with his kerchief. They stopped at the toll booth.

Jake smiled at the 40ish woman with dark hair who leaned out of the booth. She looked as if her feet hurt, but she smiled back.

"Indians get to use this road free, don't they?" Jake said.

"You tell that to the people at the other end when you got on?" she said. She showed her teeth in a wide smile. "That's a nice ring you got there. Make it yourself?"

"They didn't give me any ticket when we got on. And I did make the ring. You like it?"

"I like that turquoise. Blue is a good color." She waved them on. "Have a nice day."

They turned onto the four-lane which would take them into the city.

"I think," Tom said, "the state cop in the cruiser wasn't really asleep. I think he was watching which way we were going."

"They aren't all stupid these days," Jake said. "He saw us taking 81 south, right?"

"Right. No one following us now, though."

Jake looked in the rearview mirror, then quickly swung the van to the left, crossing the divider in the center of the road and heading back towards the north. He took the exit which led to the road around the city.

"Unless they got a chopper up top, we're okay for now."

"What happened next," Tom said, "is that one morning Harold Buffalo was just gone. They found his pillows rolled up under his blankets and even the dogs couldn't pick up his scent. They looked everywhere and couldn't find a trace. He was gone that day and all that night. But next morning we looked up towards the top of the mountain above the prison just at dawn and we saw the light of the fire and the smoke rising. It took them the better part of the day to work their way up there. They found him still sitting in front of the fire where he had been sitting to pray and greet the dawn. 'It is a good day,' he said. Then he said, 'We are going to have a sweat lodge in Fort Grant.' Everybody had seen his fire and knew what was happening, so they hardly even beat him before they brought him back down. By now the reporters from Tucson had come to the prison to get the story and they'd seen the fire, too. When they took him in to the warden, Harold told the man he knew how to get out without anyone seeing him. He could do it whenever he wanted. He could teach other men right now who knew how to do it. He told them that. Then he said, 'Sir, we want to have a sweat lodge.' Three days later, we had our first sweat."

They had bypassed the city now and they left the four-lane for a smaller road, then turned onto one of dirt which wound through the hills. The vegetation was thick and close to the road's edge. A rabbit crossed in front of them, then a raccoon. Jake slowed the blue van. They were passing a roadside dump where car bodies and garbage were strewn.

"Indian recycling station," Tom said. He took the crushed ginger ale can out of the litter bag and tossed it. It spun through the air and bounced off the cracked side of an old GE refrigerator.

"If I was a state cop," Jake said, "I would set up a little roadblock at the edge of the reservation. Maybe around the next corner where this runs back into the state road." He slowed the van down to a stop and set the emergency brake.

Tom took the duffel bag out of the back. He slung it over his shoulder. "Well," he said, patting the side of the van, "they won't have to walk far to find this. So long, Big Blue."

"They're going to catch us," Jake said. He had picked up a long stick from the roadside and was whittling carefully at it with the long knife he'd taken from the sheath at his side. The turquoise ring glinted as his hand moved with small, sure strokes.

"Not before we get to the mountain top," Tom said. It was impossible to see his eyes behind the dark glasses, but Jake knew they were hard and black and laughing.

"Yes," Jake said. "It is good to go home." They moved together into the trees.

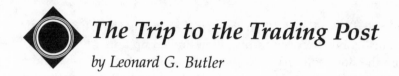

The Trip to the Trading Post
by Leonard G. Butler

The coyote had gotten into the herd without being seen either by himself or the dogs. The sheep were scattering in every direction. The lambs were no match for the speed of the coyote. It was playing with them, biting each one as it passed by, leaving a trail of dying lambs as it ran about. Why didn't the dogs go after it, he thought. He picked up a handful of rocks and ran toward the coyote. He threw a rock as hard as he could, striking the coyote on the back. It stopped running and looked at him. It began walking toward him. He was calling the dogs to help him. To his surprise the dogs ran toward the intruder and gathered behind it, and they all started coming toward him. He was throwing rocks as fast as he could and backing up. The animals began running toward him now, he turned and ran, hearing the cries of the pack behind him.

Dle ii awoke with a start and a muffled cry in his throat. He reached over and felt Bo ii's arm and he could hear him snoring softly. He was only dreaming. He glanced up and out the hogan door. The eastern horizon was orange-red and he knew the sun would soon be shining where he now lay. Looking about inside, he saw that his sisters were still asleep. The mattress where his mother slept was empty, with the blankets neatly folded. He knew without looking that his father was up and had left the hogan.

He lay still pretending he was asleep. He heard his mother come back in. He was squinting, looking through his eye lashes which made things blurry, but he could see what was going on. His father returned and spoke to his mother. Dle ii heard his father ask what they needed from the trading post.

A bolt of lighting went through him as he tried to lay still. The trading post! He felt like jumping up right then and ask if he could go; it took all his will power to pretend to wake up slowly. He yawned and moved over onto his side. His mother and father were still talking together and not paying attention to his little act. Slowly he kicked the blanket off with his legs and sat up. He had pulled the blanket off of Bo ii, who grabbed it and pulled it back and over his head, still asleep.

Dle ii rubbed his eyes and was looking around. His father glanced at him and told him to go out and wash his face. Was that a hint that he could go? He obeyed without hesitation. He sprang to his feet and practically ran out the door. The air was still cool as the sun came over the horizon. Dle ii looked to the southeast and could see the tops of the tall cottonwood trees which lined the road to the trading post. It seemed close by but he knew it was a long walk, and that his father wanted an early start before the sun got too high. He quickly splashed water on his face and grabbed the towel to dry.

He was back in the hogan, went to the mattress where he had slept and began to fold it up. He heard his father ask his mother what was wrong with him. Dle ii knew he had to be asked more than once to fold up his bedding, but not today. He was wishing his father would mention the trip to the trading post again so he could ask if he could go.

His father sat back against the wall and waited for the morning meal. Dle ii sat back and imitated his father. In his mind he was already on his way to the trading post. He could hear his mother's voice, but he was already halfway there. He was startled when he heard his father's voice; he was back in the hogan.

His father was telling him to go out and bring in some wood chips for the fire. He was outside in an instant and ran to the wood pile. The dogs came running up to him. Dle ii looked at them suspiciously, wondering whether to trust them or not. He was in a good mood; he decided to forgive them for what they had done in his dream. He pet each one, then rolled them onto their back, grabbing a leg and spinning them like a top. He remembered what he had been sent out for, picked up the chips and ran back to the hogan, dropping half of them on the way.

His father had awakened everyone and they were folding their bedding when he returned inside. His mother had warmed up the beans left over from the night before and had made fresh bread. Dle ii poured himself some tea, put two spoonfuls of sugar into it. He tore off a piece of hot bread and dunked it into the tea.

He kept glancing at his father during the meal, expecting him to mention the trip to the trading post. Bo ii, sitting next to Dle ii, was talking to him, but he wasn't paying attention to him. His father ate silently, only mentioning the sheep and the condition of the watering hole. Everyone finished eating and his sisters began clearing the dishes. He heard his father speak to his sister, Belle, asking her if she still wanted the shoes that were at the trading post. She said yes she did, and asked if they were going to walk down today. His father nodded yes, telling her to get ready.

Dle ii saw his chance, but before he could speak, Bo ii asked if he could go. He could have hit his brother. His father told Bo ii to take the sheep out, and to clean out the watering hole. Dle ii was not sure if he should ask to go now. His father looked at him. He did ask. What about me? Can I go? Bo ii poked him in the ribs, saying that he was always getting to go places. His father said yes, he could go.

91

Bo ii ran out of the hogan. Dle ii followed him, catching up with him near the sheep corral. He tried to console his brother by saying he would bring back some candy, and maybe some pop. He would ask his father to buy some caps for their cap guns. Bo ii went about removing the gate to the corral, not saying a word. Dle ii running out of things to say, returned to the hogan. His mother called him over and brushed his hair. She reached two fingers into a jar, then smeared the vaseline on his face and hands. His face was now shiny from the grease. Dle ii didn't like the vaseline or the way his mother treated him; that was for babies, not him.

His father calling out, was walking down the hill. Belle was not far behind him. Dle ii dashed out the door and caught up with the two in no time.

The air was calm and cool with not a cloud in the clear blue sky. Dle ii knew it would be a very long hot walk back home, but he would enjoy the trip down. He pretended to run into Belle. She took a poke at him but he easily dodged her fist.

He ran past her and caught up with his father. He asked him what they were going to buy at the trading post. He only replied, "Things." Dle ii asked if he would buy some caps for their cap guns. His father said, "Maybe." He took that to mean yes. He ran ahead picking up rocks and throwing them at nothing in particular.

He glanced back up the hill and could see Bo ii walking slowly behind the herd of sheep. He felt sorry for his little brother, but he thought they would be playing together later in the day, and they could share any candy that their father bought for them.

His sister, Anne, staying home too, would be helping his mother with chores around the hogan. He knew his mother would be weaving most of the day. She had made the rug which his father now carried in the white canvas bag. It would be sold for things which they needed.

The path to the trading post was plainly visible and Dle ii ran further ahead. There would be a water hole up ahead, and they would soon be walking in the shade of the tall cottonwood trees. He sat down to rest and wait for his father and sister to catch up.

He looked down toward the water hole and could see two horses grazing near by. In the direction of the trading post he could see a narrow column of smoke rising above the trees. The air was calm and the smoke was slowly going straight up. He glanced back toward the hogan but could not see it from where he sat.

His father walked past him. Belle came by and took another poke at him. He pretended to be hit rolling over into the sand. He jumped back up, running past the two, down the hill to the water hole. The horses, startled, ran a short distance, stopped and turned back, looking at him.

He found the small rusted can in a nearby bush and went over and drank a full can of water. He didn't want to drink too much, he would have a cold sweet bottle of pop when they reached the trading post. His father came up, and he handed the can to him.

Dle ii walked over to a small rock and sat down. Belle was now drinking from the can; his father sat down to rest. Belle went over and sat down by her father. She looked at Dle ii and stuck out her tongue. He only gazed back at her, not wanting his father to see him making faces. Just because she was getting new shoes today she was rubbing it in.

He didn't mind though, he was on his way to the trading post, he would probably get the caps for his gun. What else mattered? His father rose and started out again.

Dle ii tried to sneak up on Belle, to pay her back for sticking out her tongue at him, but she was too close to her father. He would get back at her later.

His father was taking long strides, Dle ii thought they would be at the store in no time. He had to run sometimes to keep up. Belle, who was not much taller than he, seemed to keep up with their father easily. He was still excited about the trip, but he was getting tired. He shouldn't have run as much as he did.

He was looking ahead, expecting to see the houses which surrounded the trading post. All he could see were the cottonwood trees and sage brush. It was warming up quickly, he could feel the sweat on the back of his neck. He was falling further behind, but his legs didn't feel like running any more.

He heard Belle call him, telling him to hurry up. He slowly began to jog, he didn't want to upset his father. He caught up to Belle, asking her how much further it was. She said they were almost there. His sister was giving him encouragement; he thought he would forget about getting back at her for the face she made at him at the water hole.

He glanced up at the tall figure of his father, who was still taking long strides, and didn't seem to be slowing down at all. Looking past his father he glimpsed one of the houses, he knew it was only a short distance now.

The trading post was made of grey rock and timber. It had a squeaky screen door that would close with a bang each time it was opened. Dle ii could hear the door before he could see it. They rounded the corner of the store, he noticed several people sitting on the ground in the shade. His father was talking and shaking hands with one of the men. He and Belle stopped, waiting for their father. Dle ii wished they would talk later, he wanted to go inside. Their father opened the door and entered; he and Belle followed him in.

Dle ii blinked and looked about. It seemed dark inside compared to the bright sunshine outside. Their father was talking to a white man standing behind the counter. He couldn't quite hear what they were saying, but suddenly the white man let out a very loud laugh, slapping the counter. Why did they have to be so noisy he thought.

The counter went completely around the inside of the store. Several people were on the other side. Near the door a lady was buying some flour. She would point and say what she wanted and the person behind the counter would go and get the item. Dle ii wondered why they could not go behind the counter to get what they wanted themselves.

His father motioned Belle over to him, she walked over and took something from his hand. She called Dle ii softly, he walked over to her. She had the lid of the pop machine open, putting in the coins her father had given to her. She asked him what he wanted. Dle ii looked inside the machine, feeling the cool air on his face.

He stood staring into the machine. He wanted them all. The bright red one, the orange one, the green one, and the one that made lots of bubbles in the mouth, root beer. Belle grabbed him by the arm, telling him to choose one. He pointed to the orange one. Belle reached in and moved the bottle down the metal channel over to a latch which made a loud clack when she lifted the bottle out.

She handed him the bottle, putting more coins into the machine. She pulled out the red one, leaning over to open the bottle. She inserted the top of the bottle into a box, the cap popped off. She reached for Dle ii's bottle, he jumped back, holding the bottle to his chest with both hands. He wanted to open it himself.

He inserted the top of the bottle into the box, but could not open the bottle. Belle said something and walked off. He was swallowing as he looked at the orange pop, cold to his hands. On the third try he opened the bottle. He took two big swallows and took a deep breath, not wanting to drink it all at once.

His father had the rug out on the counter and was still talking to the noisy white man. Belle was at one of the cases looking at the scarves on the other side of the glass. Dle ii walked over to one of the counters noticing knives which were neatly lined up in rows. He knew his father had one similar to the one with the black handle which he didn't allow the children to use. Dle ii thought about asking his father to buy him a new knife. His father would not let him use the one that he carried; why would he be willing to buy a new one for him? Dle ii settled on getting his caps and some candy.

Dle ii looked up to see another white man looking down at him with a frown. He stared back up at the man, but the man did not look away.

Why was he staring at him? He couldn't steal anything, everything was behind glass.

Dle ii turned and walked over to where Belle was looking into another case. He glanced back to the white man who was still looking at him. He thought about telling his father, but he wasn't being hurt in any way. The white man was only being impolite. He didn't think his father would do anything about that.

Dle ii turned his back on the man, asking Belle which shoes she was going to get. She looked up and pointed to a wall which had many shoes on display, and said, "That one." Dle ii looked at her, but she was already looking into the case again. Maybe she was upset because he wanted to open the pop himself.

Dle ii walked over near his father, listening to find out what the two men were talking about. They were talking money, but he didn't know how much. The noisy white man walked over to a machine on the counter, pushing some buttons on top, a drawer opened near the bottom. The man came back over to where his father stood with his hand extended. The white man counted out some numbers, handing his father the money. Dle ii did not know how much money his father received, but it seemed like a lot.

His father turned and called Belle. She came over, the white man lifted up part of the counter, and his father and sister went behind the counter. His father told him to stay. He watched as the three walked over to where the shoes were displayed. Dle ii felt alone on this side of the counter. He nervously looked over to where the impolite white man was standing. The man was busy helping an old man who was pointing at something behind the counter. Dle ii walked over to where he could see his father, feeling a little more comfortable being able to see him.

Belle was seated on a small stool, with the white man taking down boxes and showing her the shoes inside. Dle ii wished she would make up her mind so his father would return to his side of the counter.

Dle ii thought about the caps. He knew they were over by the knives, but he didn't want to go over there. He would wait for his father and go over with him. The impolite white man would not stare at him as long as the man had someone like his father to talk to. His father was taller than the man behind the counter, and just that thought made him feel better.

Dle ii was lost in his thoughts when Belle poked him in the back. Startled, he almost dropped the bottle in his hands. He made a face but did not say anything to her. She had a box wrapped with a string under her arm. Dle ii looked for his father, noticing him back from behind the counter. He went over to him.

His father was pointing and asking for different items of food which were brought to the counter in front of him. Dle ii pulled on his father's pant leg, but his father did not pay attention to him. His father finally looked down at him, reached into his pocket, handing Dle ii some coins. He told Dle ii to get his caps, and to hurry; they were about ready to leave.

Dle ii looked at the coins in his hand. He didn't know how much he had, or if he had enough to buy the caps. This wasn't going the way he wanted. He would have to go over to the impolite white man and ask him to get the caps for him. He didn't even want to talk to the man, but he wanted the caps; he had promised his brother. He looked at Belle who was looking at him. Maybe she would get the caps for him. He saw a smile on her face, and he knew she was enjoying his discomfort and would not help him. The items were being added up. Quickly looking back to his father, Dle ii knew he didn't have much time. He took the remaining swallow of his pop with difficulty, stepping out toward the counter with the knives. He clutched the coins tightly in his hand, feeling the sweat in his palm.

Dle ii was almost to the counter when he looked up; the man was looking directly at him. He froze in his tracks, unable to move. He swallowed hard and stepped up to the counter.

The way the man was looking down at him, he felt even smaller than he was. His hand was trembling as he reached out to point to the caps he wanted. The white man was enjoying himself, he thought. Dle ii pointed to the caps again, attempting to say, "Caps." His throat was dry; all he heard was a squeak.

The white man said loudly, "What?" This time he managed to say a little louder what he wanted. The man went over reaching inside the case, asking Dle ii, "How many?" He didn't know. How much money did he have? He weakly held up one finger. The man brought over a package wrapped in plastic. Dle ii could see five rolls of caps inside.

Dle ii reached up above the counter with his hand open to show the man the coins. The man picked out some coins, handing him the package. Dle ii didn't want to look at the man again. He felt there were still some coins in his hand, he lowered his arm and saw two coins still in his palm. He smiled, putting the caps in his pocket. He quickly looked up at the man, who was standing there smiling down at him.

Dle ii's eyes got big, embarrassed, he spun on his heels, running over to his father. From that safe distance he looked back at the man who was still smiling. Dle ii didn't want to smile back. He lowered his head inspecting his shoes.

His father lifted the full canvas bag over his shoulder and started for the door. Belle was close behind. Dle ii ran in front of her, almost running into the back of his father's legs. He wanted to get out of there.

Dle ii ran past his father, around the corner of the store, up the road, and into the shade of a cottonwood. He opened his fist and saw two silver colored coins in his palm. He would ask his mother how much it was when he got home. He stuffed the coins into his pocket which was already full of string, matches, rocks, and toy cars. He waited for his father and sister, letting them pass by. He would give them a head start.

He pulled the caps out of the other pocket, looking at them. Five rolls! He and Bo ii would have a good pretend fight with their guns. They would have to make them last at least more than one day.

The candy! He had forgotten the candy. He looked at the white bag on his father's shoulder. He hoped there was some candy inside it. Bo ii would really be mad at him if there wasn't. He had some money left over, but he wasn't about to go back inside the store. He put the caps back into his pocket, running after his father and sister.

The leaves of the cottonwoods hung limply in the hot dry air without even the hint of a breeze. The only sound was his breathing, and the sound of their footsteps on the hard ground. Dle ii thought he could hear the sound of a plastic bag rubbing the inside of the canvas bag with his father's every step. He didn't want to ask him about the candy. He was certain that his father would remember Bo ii and Anne.

Dle ii could feel the coolness each time they entered the shade of a cottonwood, then the heat when they moved into the sunshine. He was wondering if Bo ii would have brought the sheep in by the time they got back. He remembered he hadn't seen Bo ii carrying the lunch sack that they usually carried, this morning.

He would eat then take the sheep back out later this afternoon, then split up the caps with Bo ii. He stumbled, nearly falling to the ground; he saw Belle run ahead up behind their father. He realized that she had tried to trip him while he was daydreaming about the rest of the day. Dle ii wasn't thinking about any revenge until now.

He still didn't want to upset his father. He followed behind, seeing Belle walking ahead glancing back at him. She was making sure he didn't sneak up on her. They were getting close to the waterhole. After that there would be no shade the rest of the way home.

Dle ii, slowly tip-toeing, began running. He quietly ran past his father, then at full speed ran past Belle, not touching her. She yelled out and spun around in the path. He kept running, laughing to himself. He would think of something good to do to her; maybe a lizard.

He reached the water hole, getting the same can out of the bush. Dle ii took a can full and poured it over his head. He got another full can gulping and swallowing each mouthful loudly. The next canful he drank slowly, holding the water in his mouth. If his mother were with them, he could take the chance of teasing his sister, but not with his father. He had a wide leather belt on and didn't hesitate to take it off to whip an unruly boy on the leg.

He would rather wait until they got home; he would get his chance. Dle ii reached out his arm toward Belle as she came up, trying to hand her the water can. She made a wide circle around him going to the other side of the water hole. She kneeled and drank from her cupped hands, keeping an eye on him. She patted water on her head and wiped her face.

His father came up and set the canvas bag down. Dle ii handed him the can. His father drank half a can of water, pouring the rest inside his felt hat, working the water into the felt. Taking a deep breath he sat down.

Dle ii asked him if he bought some candy. His father looked at him. He didn't know if he should ask again. His father finally said yes, he did buy some, but he wasn't going to open it until they got home. Dle ii was relieved. At least Bo ii would get candy along with the caps.

Since his father was packing the full canvas bag, they rested longer this time. Dle ii took out an old metal toy car out of his pocket. It didn't have any wheels or paint on it any more. He couldn't remember where he had gotten it. He made a few roads in the sand where he sat. He didn't make any noise, just moved the toy along the previous tracks he had made. In his mind he was making the sound of a car.

Dle ii looked over at Belle sitting under a wild date tree. She returned his look, wondering what he was thinking of doing to her for trying to trip him. She would have to be on her toes the rest of the day. She now regretted the attempt to trip her brother. She would not rest now.

Dle ii was about to make more roads in the sand, when his father put his hat on and got up. He checked the tie on the bag then hoisted it over his shoulder. Dle ii was already on the way, anxious to get home now.

He was getting hungry, wondering about what was in the canvas bag. He knew his mother would open one of the cans and prepare something they did not have often. His mouth was watering at the thought.

Dle ii began the climb up the sandy hill but didn't stay ahead for long. His father passed him up the long hill. Dle ii looked back at his sister. Belle was holding her long skirt with one hand, holding the box in the other, taking small steps in the sand. He wondered how she could wear those clothes in this heat. The water he had put on his head was gone, replaced with sweat. It was running down his cheeks; he wiped his face with his hand.

He looked up in time to see the top of his father's hat disappear over the top of the hill. He made his legs move faster, using his hands to crawl up the remainder of the hill. He reached the top, seeing his father moving away toward the next hill. Dle ii looked back down, Belle was almost to the top. He started walking slowly, holding back to make sure Belle made it up the hill.

Glancing back again, Belle was on top looking at him. She was waiting for him to move further away. Dle ii couldn't understand why she didn't want to get close to him. His father was about halfway up the next hill. From there it was possible to see the hogan.

Dle ii started to walk a little faster. He looked up again to see his father disappear over the top of the hill. If the dogs were back home, they would begin barking at him. Bo ii would know they would be home soon.

He was almost to the top of the hill when he heard the dogs barking. Good, Bo ii was back home. He would have a surprise to give to his little brother. Belle was taking her time, stopping now and again looking about.

Dle ii made it to the top of the hill, seeing the hogan in the distance. Bo ii was standing on a small hill looking in his direction. His father was almost home with the sun shining brightly on the white canvas bag. He saw Bo ii run off the hill toward his father. The dogs were close behind but made a wide circle around the man. They knew better than to get too close to him.

Bo ii reached his father and was looking up at him walking beside him. Dle ii knew just what questions his brother was asking, and he smiled. He had been left at home many times and had asked the same questions of his mother and father when they returned home.

Dle ii, looking up, saw his father enter the shade house which was next to the hogan. He knew there would be cool water inside; his father would drink, then begin unpacking the bag.

One of the dogs noticed him now and began barking. He whistled. The dog's ears went up and started to run toward him. The other dogs came out of the shade. They too ran toward him. He thought about his dream again, but thought it was bright daylight; he couldn't possibly be dreaming now. It was too hot for dreams.

The dogs reached him and tried to jump up on him. Dle ii pushed them away, running slowly toward the shade house. Belle was still taking her time, looking into the box she carried. He made it to the shade house, going straight to the water bucket.

Dle ii took the dipper, dripping water down the front of his shirt, making loud noises with each swallow. He knew Anne didn't like him drinking water this way, but he didn't care right now. He was feeling good again. With his mother around he could tease his sisters.

Bo ii came over asking him if he got them. He motioned him with his eyes, which was their secret signal. Dle ii looked at Anne who was glaring at him. He raised his eyebrows several times at her; she looked away with disgust. He laughed to himself, walking out and toward the corral.

Bo ii, right behind him, was asking all kinds of questions. He reached into his pocket, showing him the caps. Bo ii's eyes got big, and he asked how much they had cost. Dle ii replied that he didn't know. His father had given him some money, and he had bought them.

They reached the corral where Dle ii ripped the plastic off the caps. He took two rolls, giving them to Bo ii. He took two more rolls, putting them on top of a log on the corral. From the last role he gave one end to Bo ii, telling him to back up, and they unrolled the caps. He then folded them in half. Dle ii tore the roll at the crease, giving half of it to Bo ii. Now they each had two and a half rolls of caps.

Dle ii remembered the two coins he had. He still didn't know how much it was. He took them out of his pocket and showed Bo ii. He said that this was left over after he bought the caps. Dle ii put the coins together; they were the same size, having the same pictures on them. They must be worth the same amount, he thought. He handed one of the coins to Bo ii, putting the other back into his pocket.

Dle ii asked his little brother if they were even now. Bo ii said no. "No! Why not!" Bo ii reached into one of his pockets and handed Dle ii a piece of candy his father had given him. Bo ii said, now, they were even.

They smiled at one another and began walking toward their lookout hill. Each placed an arm around the other's shoulder. Dle ii said he had a story to tell about his trip to the trading post today. They both laughed, each with a mouthful of candy.

Loretta

by Jack D. Forbes

Jesse found a good place to sit, where he could watch people passing to and from a trading post, a Chapter House, and a small cafe.

In such places he would get out his sketch-pad and try to capture the things he was seeing or, more correctly, the feelings he was experiencing.

A group of Navajo school girls came out of the store. They looked at Jesse with friendly, happy eyes, and then passed on, allowing sounds of laughter to drift to his ears.

He put aside his drawing pad and began writing a letter to himself, trying to save for another day the impressions racing through his mind.

"Beautiful Navajo girls. Skin so smoothly dark walnut brown magically mountain honey-colored. Do you all taste as sweet as you look? No deodorants for Navajo girls, no strong smells to be erased, only smokey sage-juniper-pinon tinged aromas. Black, glossy-lustered soft hair streaming, cascading, falling or wrapped, proudly, on to the head. Why are high cheek-bones so attractive? Why do they even make blonde European girls look better?

Navajo girls' eyes, Indian girls' eyes, all different shaped, some almond, some full and round, but it isn't the shape. Coming out of them is a warmth, a joy, a sheer pleasure in being an admired, free, proud, useful, skilled, nurturing, strong, independent, "spoken for" woman.

Every Navajo girl, every Indian girl, is already spoken for, at birth, before birth. The universe, the Great Creator, Changing Woman, the plants, the earth, Corn-Mother, all life, everything has made a place for the Native girl. Sensing her power, sensing her sexuality, sensing her established place as a creator and sustainer of life and of beauty, she walks in beauty, dropping as she goes petals of quiet laughter, blossoms of starlight smiles and whole flowers of shielded sidelong glances.

To hear a Native girl sing. Not just vapid song from the front of the mouth. Deep and high, nasal, earth-power singing, like the fado, or the flamenco in depth but sincere, open, without the decadence of corrupted civilizations. Gypsy beauty but pure and unpainted. Straight-forward, arrow-point sharp but soft still, womanly. One could listen for days without

101

awareness of time. Nights could fly by and one could grow old without caring, such is their power if they wanted to enchant that way.

When a Navajo girl grasps your belt and takes you to dance . . . To be with a proud, self-aware woman. One cannot use such a girl wrongly, unless one is truly deranged. They are too precious.

Navajo girls talking. Glottal stops and clicks at the end of words. Liquid flowing, not sugar water but some kind of melodious dignified powerful soothing way of talking. Don't ever lose your accent Navajo girl! If you do I'll leave you. Don't ever stop talking in Navajo the way you do. Don't ever learn to sing sugary-empty. Husky-nasal voiced song, power-female talking, don't let it go.

Mother Earth-female-upright walking, slim and full-bosomed, dancing, always dancing, running-dancing, walking-dancing, sitting-dancing, head up high, looking the world over, loving men.

Indian girls are man-lovers. They birth men, they care for men, they are not afraid of them. Unabused, self-assured, esteemed, they can love fully. Traditional Indian men must be good to, sensitive to their women's power, gifts, they give too. But it isn't the women on my mind," wrote Jesse. "It is their power-beauty that draws me."

Slight, small but they are not toys. They are not tanks either, with guns blazing like some other women. Real, authentic, filled with vital force of love itself, soft like wind but hard-carving wearing down rocks.

It is easy to fall in love with a Navajo girl, but is it fair to take her away? Shouldn't she raise more Navajo girls? If you take her with you what can she raise, away from other Navajos? Do you want to destroy that flow of generations — do you want to interrupt the very thing that grips you, bring it to a halt? Please, make sure that more Indian girls are made, thought Jesse. Let them go on and on into the future, models, prototypes of womanness after all the others have disappeared into the ocean of empty middle-class wives with its thrown-up waves of rebellious, man-hating feminists."

Indian girls, even Navajo girls, *could* be changed, as Jesse had seen. Alcohol and poverty and hopelessness could create the cunning survivors of Gallup and the border towns, or the old ladies joining their men in connubial winoships. But in Window Rock and Fort Defiance Jesse had also met the products of BIA-missionary training, hard, cold, bitter-eyed de-Navajoized ladies behind desks with their hair curled and done up in fancy World War II white styles.

Jesse had hated Indian women to do up their hair. How could they take their beautiful long black hair, reflecting the light like gleaming obsidian, and torture it with curlers or whatever to make it into something else? But the BIA and the missionaries taught them to hate their

Indianness and long, straight black hair was one of the signs that had to be erased.

Still, that only made Jesse appreciate Indian girls more. If there had been no BIA, no missionaries no hard-eyed white trader's wives, no corrupted Indians, then he wouldn't have thought that much about unspoiled Navajo girls. He wouldn't have appreciated them so much, at least not consciously, because there would have been nothing to contrast them with. And so even an evil has some value. At least it makes you appreciate the good that much more, that is, if you're still free enough to know the difference.

A few days later Jesse went to a dance out in the country with a friend of his, a Navajo who had moved back to the reservation from Los Angeles. Fred Yazzie, a young man in his twenties, was sure of himself at the gathering and danced quite a bit but Jesse kept to the margins, listening to the singing and watching the other people intently but unobtrusively.

Every so often he would notice Fred dancing with a girl or talking with a group of men. Several times different men came up to Jesse and they would talk a little but the girls seemed to stay together in small groups except when dancing. Jesse looked at many of them but when they noticed him they turned their glances shyly away or laughed a little and talked with their friends. One woman, however, looked at him several times. She was, perhaps, a little bit older than most of the girls. Dark brown, with markedly high cheekbones, she lowered her eyes whenever he looked at her but nonetheless shot him veiled glances that told of her awareness of his interest. He called her "Red Skirt" to himself, but she disappeared from view before he could get up the courage to walk over her way.

Disappointed, Jesse turned his attention to other portions of the crowded scene, until distracted by a hand on his shoulder. Fred was at his side, saying "You ought to go out there. Get in the line-up. There's a girl who wants to dance with you." He was grinning. Jesse said "Are you kidding me? I'm scared to go out there." "Go on. You got to. It's the rule. You can't just stand around all night. You got to make the ladies happy, Jesse."

So Fred kind of shoved Jesse out and he went, not reluctantly but somewhat nervous at the idea of waiting to see if a girl would pick him as a dance partner.

He didn't have long to wait, though, as "Red Skirt" came up to him, self-confidently but without boldness. "You have to dance or give me some money," she said as her hands grasped his belt. Her eyes frankly and good-humoredly examined him, carefully noting his reaction. Jesse, on his part, was very pleased. "I sure ain't goin' to give you any money."

So they danced arm in arm. Jesse had learned the steps at pow-wows but at first he felt very stiff compared with her confidence and her effortless movements. When the dance was finished he asked her to dance again and gradually he became more relaxed, becoming increasingly aware of her body against his arm and of her hands in his.

"My name's Jesse. What's yours?" "Loretta," she said. "I'm Fred's sister. We belong to the same clan." "Did he ask you to dance with me?" queried Jesse. "No," she replied emphatically, with a suppressed smile on her lips, "I asked him to get you out here so I could find out why you were staring at me so hard." "I'm sorry, I didn't mean to look at you so, but you're very pretty and I just couldn't help it, Red Skirt."

"Red Skirt! Is that my name now?"

"Yes, that's what I called you, in my mind, when I was looking at you."

"You like me," she stated.

"Yes."

"I like you. What tribe are you?"

And so they talked and danced, losing track of the time and keeping together in between dances to show that they wanted to stay together. He could smell her body by then, and his arm sometimes touched her breast as they danced. His hands became sweaty and he was a little embarrassed but Loretta didn't seem to mind.

"You have a woman?" she asked.

"No, not now. I'm alone, looking for one though, if I can find a good one like you."

"I'm not good," she smiled. "I'm a bad woman. My nose is too big, face too thin."

"I'm not goin' to play any games, Red Skirt, you're beautiful so don't try to say things like that. I like your face, all of it."

She was pleased.

"You're staying with Fred, ey, but it's so crowded there."

"Yeah, I'll probably have to start camping out again. That's what I've been doing. Sleeping with the snakes and coyotes."

"How long you goin' to be around here? What are you going to do?"

"I'm not sure. It depends on what I find, if I get a job. The truth is, I want to find out about Navajo women. That's my secret mission."

"Hey, you'll never find that out, there's too much to learn. But a good teacher would help. That's what you need."

"Can you recommend one?"

"Ey, there's an old lady I know, 80 years old. She's old and wrinkled and almost blind but she would be happy to teach you."

Red Skirt laughed. Many couples were drifting away now, going out into the darkness or disappearing among the trucks and camps. She took Jesse's arm and pulled him gently and they wandered off too, finding a place to sit beyond a juniper tree.

"I like you," she whispered. "You can stay with me if you'll be good to me, treat me gentle and nice."

Jesse kissed her and gently caressed her breasts. "I should tell you," she said, "I have two babies, two little boys. Maybe that would bother you."

"That won't bother me," replied Jesse. "I like kids. I just don't want a husband there."

Red Skirt smiled. "No, my husband's gone. I haven't got a man now."

And so it all fell into place. Jesse moved in with Loretta Begay in her little government built house in Chinle. She worked in the kitchen of the school cafeteria while a clan sister nearby watched her children.

Loretta's husband had abandoned her, temporarily or permanently no one knew, and had gone off to find a job in Denver, people said. She was a high school graduate but that only meant that she had studied up to ninth-grade work. She had learned to type a little but had ended up in the school cafeteria because she had no other skills and, with two babies, had no thought of going on to college. She really wanted to go home to her family out in another part of the reservation, but since she had a job and the homeplace was overcrowded that was out of the question.

Loretta wouldn't have stayed in Chinle, however, if she had been completely alone. But she had her clan-sister who lived nearby and some other relatives, such as Fred, who could be called upon for help in an emergency. Nonetheless, she deeply missed her family and home and often cried to herself at night when she felt depressed and lonely.

The school paid very little. Loretta managed, though, to send her family some money every so often and she saved what she could. Her dream was to save enough so that she could buy some sheep and a truck and move back home. She didn't like Chinle, especially where she was living. The government houses were square and poorly built. Hot in the summer, cold in the winter, with bathrooms that stopped working and ceilings that fell in. There were no streets either, or yards, all erased long ago by cars and trucks driving wherever they wanted to. Everything was mud when it rained and dust when it didn't rain.

But the people survived and Loretta was one of them. She tried to beautify her house with what Navajo blankets and rugs she could afford to keep (and they could also be sold in an emergency). She had put up magazine pictures and a few photographs and, here and there, pieces of wood, herbs, knick-knacks, and beadwork. Her furniture consisted of a few chairs, an old table, a radio, two mattresses, and several packing crates used for books, magazines, toys, newspapers, and clothing.

Loretta usually cooked outside, on the shady side of the house in the summer, to save on fuel bills and because that was the way she had been raised. Having no refrigerator, she had to use mostly canned goods or dried food anyway. Still she had to go to the store almost every day because, not having a car, she couldn't carry much at any one time. She didn't really mind that since there wasn't much in the way of excitement in Chinle. Going to the store was a diversion, a chance to meet friends or to look over things that you might want to buy one day.

Loretta hoped her husband would come back someday but she didn't dwell on it in her mind. She thought far more about her family and her babies than she did of him. Other men had briefly known her but she hadn't found anyone she really liked until Jesse had laid down with her out there on the sand beneath the stars the night of the dance.

Loretta gambled, of course, when she let Jesse move in. He had no job. He had no money, so far as she knew. He would eat a lot of food. But like a lot of Indian women she was not looking for financial support or middle-class security. That never occurred to her. Instead she simply wanted to share her life, her body, her love, her nurture with a man who would be kind and gentle and would share himself with her. What happened after that would be up to the future.

Jesse, for his part, was very happy. He fell in love with Loretta and their first days together were like a honeymoon. When she was away during the day, he tackled the plumbing, borrowing tools to get the toilet and the shower working once again. He also repaired the ceiling, and after scouring the country side for logs and pieces of wood, he built a ramada near the house and gathered rocks for a better fire pit.

Perhaps he felt guilty about living off a woman's labor. But so far as Loretta was concerned he repaid her many times over. The warmth of his body at night and his caresses were enough in themselves, but on top of that he played with the boys and eased her burdens in countless little ways. Jesse usually met her as she walked home from work and helped her carry groceries. He brought the babies along too, so they could enjoy the walk.

At night, after dinner, he tried to learn Navajo. But every time Jesse tried to say something like "Dineh dish dintsa?" or whatever, Red Skirt would break into such laughter that he got discouraged. Jesse became convinced that Navajos have a secret desire to prevent outsiders from learning their language and that they use laughter to so embarrass the victim that he will give up. Nonetheless, he persisted since it seemed to entertain her and he knew, after all, that she liked him.

On their first weekend together, after carrying the laundry to a laundromat and returning the washed clothes to the house, they hiked up Canyon de Chelly loaded down with blankets, dried food, the babies, and Jesse's sleeping bag. Loretta had been up the canyon, so she was happy to show Jesse a place so important to her people's history. Jesse was elated to show her what he had seen and to learn from her what she had heard about the great Tsegi.

That night they camped together with only the darkness and the stars around them. The sound of running water and the breeze, high up among the cliffs and rocks, together made music for them, and they were content. Loretta had not been so happy for a long time and even the little boys were positively affected by Jesse's attention and the new experiences they were having.

As Loretta cuddled the babies and stared into the fire Jesse thought how wonderful she was. How nice it was to camp out with a woman who had been camping all her life, so to speak, who knew how to gather kindling for the fire, who knew how to stack the wood just right to get it burning, who knew how to cook with no utensils, and who knew how to love a man in such a way that he floated on a cloud singing, filled with warmth and tenderness, joyously becoming something wonderfully renewed at her touch.

In such a way the days and weeks went by. Jesse managed to buy some canvases and started painting. He got some beads and made a beading loom. Loretta was a good beader but she had given it up. Now she started again, working as Jesse painted. Jesse's ambition was to sell some paintings so that he could buy a sewing machine for Loretta. Then she could make clothes for herself and the boys. He also wanted her to develop her beading, sewing, and weaving so that she could better support herself if she ever lost her job.

During the day Jesse did a lot of walking, looking for wood, wire, and anything else potentially useful. As he walked about he also observed, learning a lot about the life around him. He saw how the Navajos, as vital and numerous as they were, were dominated by the white culture. The trading posts were run by whites or half-breeds who acted like whites. The signs were all in English everywhere — road signs, business signs, government signs, even tribal signs. Even the *Navajo Times* newspaper was all in English. Who could read it, he thought. Who was it printed for?

The prices in the stores were terribly high, so he understood why everybody who could drove to Gallup or other border towns to shop. It was not only an exciting diversion, it was also an economic necessity. The trading posts also had poor quality foods, lots of sugary cereals and other junk, and many times the corn flakes tasted moldy or stale. Used appliances, such as sewing machines, sold for almost as much as new ones in Los Angeles.

Jesse also observed how the white teachers and government officials lived in segregated compounds and took their money off-reservation. It was truly a colony, he thought, with everything, even the people, being sucked out by the colonizing society.

One day Jesse and Loretta hitched a ride together to Gallup in a relative's pick-up. They sold enough paintings and beadwork there to buy a used sewing machine, some toys for the boys, and some fabric for making clothes. Jesse didn't get much for his paintings. He knew he was being cheated but what could he do? He was like any other Indian artist on the reservation, helpless because he needed the money, at the mercy of the white and Mexican curio shop owners.

Jesse decided then and there to try to find a way to sell his paintings directly to the tourists if he could. On the way home, in Window Rock, Loretta joined the tribal arts and crafts guild at Jesse's suggestion and got some wool for weaving.

Because of that, Jesse could also sell some of his paintings, using Loretta's last name, at the guild's store.

Loretta had never been off the reservation, except to go to Gallup, so Jesse planned next to save up money, get a ride to Albuquerque, and maybe buy a used truck or car there. Then they could go on a grand tour, visiting her home place and seeing a lot of things that were too far away to hitchhike to.

It took a long time but finally they had enough money, crafts, and paintings to take their trip. Loretta was on vacation so they had the time.

Jesse found a used pick-up in Albuquerque, with a camper on the back. Thus royally outfitted they drove north to Santa Fe where they visited the museum, galleries, and some of Jesse's artist friends. Loretta bought quite a few things and Jesse asked her, "Don't you think you ought to save some money? Just in case." Loretta looked at him with a side-long glance and said simply, "My husband sent me a money-order two weeks ago, from Denver."

She said nothing more, and Jesse asked no further. But it brought home to him the fact that she was a married woman whose man might well return one day.

Loretta was extra-affectionate towards Jesse after that, and so they both had a good time, visiting Tesuque, San Juan, and Taos before turning west. They hiked through Mesa Verde and other ruins, although Loretta was nervous and refused to go into any of the old houses. "Someone might have died there," was all she said.

They drove to Shiprock and over to her family's home place, camping out as usual. Both very happy, they made love as ardently as when they first met and every evening around the campfire seemed so enjoyable, so relaxing, so free from worry that they hated the thought of returning to Chinle. Loretta's kinfolk were pleased to see her and Jesse was made to feel welcome. Still, he felt a little left-out because many of the older ones seemed to speak no English.

When Loretta said she would like to stay for a while longer, Jesse decided to drive back to Chinle alone. He stopped at Fred Yazzie's first and luckily so. Fred seemed a little nervous and said, "A few days ago I got a message that Loretta's husband is on his way back from Denver. He hasn't come yet, but I thought you'd want to know. He says, that he's sorry he left so suddenly but now he wants to move back. He's saved some money." Jesse felt a churning in the pit of his stomach, but he said only, "Thanks for telling me. I'll go back and tell Loretta. You can tell her husband, when he comes, that she's with her family." Jesse then went to Loretta's house and packed up all his personal things, leaving nothing to cause trouble for her.

As he drove back out to her home place he made up his mind to let her go if she wanted to return to her husband. "After all, she doesn't belong to me. I don't own her. Anyway, it's best for the kids to be with their father."

Loretta was not surprised by the news. She said, "I love you Jesse. You been real good to me and my children. But I love my husband also and he's sent me money, so I know he cares about me. I think he needs me more than you do."

So Jesse turned away from her long black hair, her firm breasts, her warm brownness, her strength, her steady nurture, turned again to resume his wandering. He said only, "You've been good to me Loretta. I love you. If he's ever mean to you, leave him and come to me. Even if I have another woman, I'll try to help you out."

A few days later, from Gallup, Jesse phoned Lucas Fixico, his old army buddy in Oklahoma. It was the first time he had established contact with any friends or relatives for months (although he had sent a long letter to Jennifer from Santa Fe before meeting Loretta and had also sent a letter to Ramona in care of her uncle and a copy in care of Ladell. But he had given no return address so there had been no replies).

Lucas was glad to hear from Jesse. He had gotten caught up in the "Indian Power" movement and was planning to go to the National Congress of American Indians convention that fall. He said, "Jesse, why don't we meet there. We can have a good time together." So Jesse agreed.

He drove south first, to Rufus Wildcat's place to pick up El Sabio. Now that he had a camper he wanted the dog with him, if El Sabio wanted to go along. The old wise-one listened carefully, examined the camper, and decided that that was what he wanted too. So together they prepared to go with a bundle of Indian posters Rufus had ordered from Ladell. Jesse called Ladell on the phone but she had no information about Ramona, so he and El Sabio departed to the north, on the road once again.

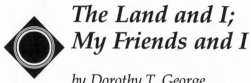

The Land and I;
My Friends and I

by Dorothy T. George

I am a Hopi man. My name is Tuvangyumptewa. I live and work as my father has done and his father has done. In the year, 1906, when the big split occurred in Old Oraibi, I took my family and resettled in Hotevilla. Times were hard, but we all managed to clear new land for farming and grazing. I am fortunate to have sheep.

The Hopi way of life has never been easy, but it always has been good. Our beliefs in the Great Spirit sustain us through the hard times. We have enough to eat and we have our ceremonies. Hopis are farmers and have always managed to grow corn.

My wife, Sehongnim, and I have raised seven children. She has been a good mother, and now she is a good grandmother to our many grandchildren. Our children are now grown and most have left the reservation. But our lives have not changed much. We still live in the house where our children were born and raised. We are getting old, but I still go to the fields and I still herd sheep. My wife is still strong and manages to raise some chili, corn, and squash in a small plot near the spring, where she gets our drinking water.

I am gone for days at a time. When I am away, she tries to chop wood, haul water, and keep our home going. There is a daughter to help now and then, and, of course, the grandchildren keep her company. But she is alone most of the time. I am alone most of the time also. As I herd sheep or work in the corn fields, I am alone with nature. Today, I am herding sheep again. There are no other sounds, only the bleating of the sheep and the tinkling of the bell on the lead sheep. It is summer, and it is hot, but is nicer than being in the cold of winter.

I take along some wool and my spinning tool. While the sheep are grazing, I sit in whatever shade I can find, and spin some yarn. The yarn I use for knitting leggings for our ceremonials. Also, I weave a blanket whenever I can find someone to herd the sheep. I have been at the sheep camp for three days, and I go home today, for my wife will be waiting.

I look at the sun and measure the distance by a landmark. The sun is low, and I know I should start home. I get my burro and begin the ride. As I ride along, I realize I should have started sooner. For I know I am only two-thirds of the way home, and it is already getting dark. I can hear my wife as she tells me each time I leave home, "Start home early; don't tarry, for you get lost easily."

I prod my burro to hurry. I feel that I am not on the right trail, so I tap my burro to turn. He refuses, but I insist. As I ride along, I look for the lights from the mesa, but I see none. Finally, I have to admit it, I am lost. I call out; it is possible that another sheepherder may be going home late. I hear no sounds. There is no one to help me, and I feel helpless.

Then I remember the teachings of my father and grandfather. I have been taught that everything is alive out here on the land. All plants and all animals have a human side. So I call out, "My Friends, I know you are out there, please help me for I know I am not on the right trail." I sit on my burro in the quiet of the night, and I wait. Then I see them — two small flickering flames. I am not afraid, for I know they will not hurt me. They position themselves in front of me, and I know they are telling me where the path is. I say to them, "I am ready." My burro is also not afraid. I urge him to go and we start for home.

As we go along, I see lights, like a village, and I realize it is the old graveyard. I see lights where I buried my uncle. As we pass, I say a silent prayer for all the people who have left us.

We go on, my friends and I. Finally, I can see the outline of the mesa, which we must climb. I know I am almost home. I say to my guides, "Thank you for your help; I know where I am. I am happy that you came to help me." As I thank them, they disappear.

As I get to the top, my grandchildren run to meet me. It is late and they have been waiting at the edge of the mesa. They were worried.

I put my burro in the corral, and I walk home with my grandchildren.

I will tell my wife of this experience, but not immediately. I will eat and I will let them tell me of their activities while I was gone; then I will tell them of my friends.

Past Due
by Virgil Link

Returning to the San Carlos Apache Reservation, Jeff first checked out the old bowling alley where he had taught himself the game. It had been converted into a community center during his absence. When he walked into the empty shell of a building, a nostalgic sensation overwhelmed him and left him emotionally disappointed and saddened. The shock of its emptiness astonished him, and he held his breath as if he had just missed a five-pin down the center of the lane. The alley's concrete floor lay exposed, its walls stood bare, its ceiling checkered from missing acoustical tiles. The only furnishings in the building were some scattered folding chairs and tables. The best game he had ever rolled had been just about where he stood. Ten strikes in a row, a feat he had never duplicated. If he had, maybe he would not be standing where he stood. He had bombed out on the tour after a couple of years. Inside Jeff felt like the old bowling alley looked. The alley had been gutted of its vital organs as though it were a discarded carcass of a skinned coyote.

Five years had elapsed since he had first left the reservation, and he returned now with the anticipation of staying. From high school, Jeff had gone directly into college at Arizona State, made its bowling team, but had never graduated. He had left school to join the tour. A decision he now regretted very much. His first year on tour was not too bad. He had won enough to pay his expenses, but then things took a downturn. He ended up having to sell arts and crafts just to continue. It came to the point where he started making more money with arts and crafts than with his bowling, so he stopped altogether. But back on the San Carlos Reservation, how ironic it was, Jeff thought. Of all the houses and all the subdivisions on the reservation, his sister had to be given a house directly next to a certain crippled man. The man confined to the wheelchair was not a stranger to him, and to spy on his activities through curtained windows had become an obsession. The presence of the man so near to where he lived aggravated a deep, latent emotion he had thought he had successfully subdued. It caused him to think maybe he had made the wrong decision about returning.

They had been friends, bowling teammates to be exact, but they had gone separate ways. He had met him at the alley and thought him to be a natural because he had a natural left-hooking ball. Once paired up, they had become an unbeatable combination everywhere they bowled

If the truth were told, his friend was the better bowler, but his friend had a problem. Jeff was not the kind of person who would knowingly give an alcoholic more money so the addict could purchase more alcohol. Yet, after months of successfully repulsing his teammate's begging for money, he had slipped him the last dollars from his wallet. He could still vividly recall the day, the mistake, the flashing lights and the money. Shortly thereafter he left for college, and he had not seen the man again until now.

He had seen the ambulance with flashing red lights pass him on the street while on his way to the bank to cash his check. A bartender, Jeff knew, was liable for his patrons if he knowingly served them alcohol beyond a reasonable limit. He had never told anyone he had given his old friend some money on that morning. He had kept his part of the accident a secret. When he heard the details of where his old friend had received a blow to the head, a sudden guilt reached out and gripped him instantly. He wanted to bash the guy who had attacked his buddy, but after some thought, he decided to vent his anger on the tribal council for being unable to irradicate bootlegging from the reservation. Reflecting on the whole experience, he later concluded it probably had been just an impulse to rid himself of his own implication in the incident. It had worked, but not totally, because he was beginning to ask why he was feeling some old familiar pangs. Still, the bootleggers continued to thrive on his reservation. An honorable anger sought restitution relentlessly until some form of justice was satisfied. Jeff reluctantly recalled how a whimsical thought of his had almost launched a campaign against the reservation bootleggers — pressuring the tribal council to pass a cease and desist order against them. He also recalled how shortly afterwards he left for college, conveniently disappearing for five years. So much for old friends and acquaintances, he thought.

Since his return, Jeff's arts and crafts productivity had drastically declined, and no wonder since he now lived next door to his conscience in a wheelchair. The unfinished materials still lay packed in boxes, and what little he had unpacked lay scattered on a work table. The table sat facing the cripple's back yard. Jeff's sand paintings also lay covered with only the first coat of background colors of beige, natural earth and greys. The foreground on all of them appeared void of any colorful images. He had not yet started the detailed drawings of Apache figures or geometrical designs. The pre-cast ceramics also remained untouched by his artistic hands. He had fallen so far behind on his work, he needed a loan from his brother to get himself on his feet again.

Generally, Apaches did not smoke, but his father had been a heavy smoker. By the time the doctors had found traces of cancer in his lungs, it had been much too late. There was no one who could do anything for him, not even the Apache medicine men who tried to arrest his malignancy. His father had died slowly and painfully. And so it was for the tribal members who drank heavily and obliviously. Undoubtedly, his old acquaintance could never recover from his misfortune and regain the use of his limbs. He would never bowl again. His old teammate had paid a horrible price, but it also amazed Jeff just how well he had prevailed against such an unspeakable tragedy. Of course, he wished his old friend had emerged unscathed, but then again, he had swindled Satan himself. He now had a wife and family, and was living comfortably and happily, something he may not have managed to achieve otherwise.

Only in the high mountains did Arizonans ever find relief from hot summers, and the San Carlos Apaches were not excluded from this certainty. It was still early morning, but it was already pushing 90 degrees, and Jeff felt the heat of the coming day bear down on him. He walked his way slowly to his brother's house trying not to work up a sweat. Suddenly, a young lady whisked by him on beautiful, brown legs. Jeff forget about keeping cool, and set out after the girl with the bobbing ponytail. It appeared to him she was headed in the same direction he was. Quickly he fell in stride beside her, but he could sense she was somewhat perturbed by his advance, and she quickened her stride. Jeff stayed right with her. Despite her coolness, her pace became more accommodating to his unconditioned body and she slowed. In the short jog to his brother's house she became more amicable, and he humored her phone number from her, also learning she was available. He would definitely check her out later.

Exhausted, Jeff collapsed against the door of his brother's house. It took more than a couple of deep breaths to regain his composure, but by then his brother opened the door with a newspaper in hand.

"If you must die, don't do it in my front yard. Come inside where we can flush you down the toilet like my son's little goldfish," his brother remarked. "I saw you staggering up to the door. I can tell you now, you're in no shape for that gal. She runs by here almost everyday. If I were you, I'd forget it. She's definitely too much woman for you. You're better off with those little fat ones who always hang around the bars at night."

"I'm not a quitter, Bro," he panted. "All I needed was her number. I can always recover. You married guys have it easy. If I don't get flushed down your toilet, I just might get to see her this weekend."

Like the sister he stayed with, his brother lived in housing provided by the federal government but administered by the Apache tribe. Once inside his brother's house, he went straight for his refrigerator. Being the laid back guy his brother was, it was conceivable he would prefer to have his refrigerator right in his livingroom, so he would not have to run back and forth to the kitchen for beers while watching television. He hoped his brother had not drunk all the beer from the weekend. His brother's family was one of the few who did not have to live on the San Carlos Reservation, but he stayed on account of his in-laws, because his wife did not want to leave. For this reason, he kept his family on the reservation along with the other Apaches in a tribal housing project. "My brother, my brother, where is all the beer?" Jeff asked while fumbling through his refrigerator. "This is Monday. You must have drunk it all. What are you going to do about Monday Night Football?"

"Beer is for drinking, not to let sit around in the refrigerator," his brother declared and then asked, "How long are you planning to stick around? You haven't given up the tour completely have you?"

"No, I don't think so," Jeff answered, "I'm just a little burned out right now. I think I'll sit it out for a season."

On the coffee table, with his brother across from him, he laid out his loan application. Jeff explained how he planned to repay the loan, a loan his brother had agreed to co-sign by collateralizing his cattle. Years ago for graduation from high school, his father had given his brother a few head of cattle to start a herd. His father had given him the same gift on his graduation, but instead of multiplying them, he had gradually cashed them in to finance his college and finally his bowling tour. His brother never went to college, instead went straight to work, saving his cattle until they grew into a small herd. "There you go little brother," his brother obliged. "I hope you don't quit the tour so soon. I haven't even seen you on television yet."

The smell of frying bacon and eggs gripped his stomach and pulled him with its hold on his nose. When he first entered, the sound of utensils and the smell of breakfast indicated Claudine was busy preparing his brother something to eat. Before they married, his brother and his wife worked at a restaurant in Tucson, and Jeff knew she could whip out a breakfast. She called them both to breakfast which made him feel good inside, but at the table, as usual, his brother buried his face in his rodeo magazine. Whenever his wife asked him something, all the response she could get was a grunt from a mouthful of bacon and eggs. "You are rude. You know that?" she objected, "I can understand it when you behave like this with my mother, but this is your brother. I cooked breakfast just for the two of you. Put your magazine away. It takes you forever to finish that magazine."

"We have finished our business," he replied. "I signed the papers. He has already told me he is not ready to quit the tour yet. What else is there to talk about? I just watched him bust his gut trying to move in on the girl from up the street. Maybe you can ask him something about her. I'm not interested."

"Well, so you like what you see, huh?" his sister-in-law asked him.

"Yuh, I got her phone number," Jeff replied to his sister-in-law.

"Maybe you can take her back on tour with you, huh?" she suggested. "I'm sure she wouldn't turn you down. It's just probably what that one is looking for. She is the talk around here. I'm sure she will be something interesting for you. Some of the things people say about her are unbelievable. I hope I haven't said too much about her already."

With a righteous gesture of disapproval and a smirk, their conversation chased his brother into the livingroom. They did not catch what he said to them, but it had something to do with gossiping. No one said anything as he left. Jeff explained to her his need for a loan from his brother, because he had fallen behind on his arts and crafts, and he had dropped out of the tour because he started making more money selling than from his bowling. He also regretted never having finished his college degree and was even thinking about completing it sometime soon. He had not heard the real story of how his old friend in a wheelchair and his fair lady had come together, and whenever he mentioned it to his brother, he always responded with something derogatory and senseless. He had put much thought into the circumstances surrounding the incident, and if there was anyone who could give him an honest answer, it was his sister-in-law. He decided to ask.

Boldly he looked at her, gathered his thoughts and asked her his first question. His inquiry provoked a strong response from his brother instead, his first in about a half-hour. He had sneaked in to eavesdrop on their conversation. His brother spewed a long string of familiar profanity, and for his vulgar opinions his sister-in-law kicked him hard from where she sat, making him choke on his cigarette. He demanded to know why she kicked him. "It's none of your business, Mike," she scolded. "If you can't say anything nice about someone, don't say anything. Get back into the other room and read your dumb magazine. I'm glad our kids aren't here to hear you." Nothing was said between them until Mike finally left the kitchen. But before he would leave, he walked over to the coffee pot and refilled his cup first.

"When he was laid up in the hospital, he met his lady," his sister-in-law smiled, delighted in the story she was about to tell. "She was his nurse. When he was finally discharged, they were married and she returned home with him. How about that? I've met her, and she is very nice. Why would she marry a cripple, right? She really loves him, Jeff. But nobody wants to believe it. They have a beautiful girl called Rebecca.

117

She comes over and plays with our kids. She has curly hair, big brown eyes and she's a doll." His sister-in-law became animated and squirmed delightfully at the thought of the little girl. He understood why, because he had seen Rebecca from a distance. She whispered across the table to Jeff how she wished they could have a curly-haired little girl like Rebecca.

"You really believe that?" Jeff thoughtlessly asked, inciting an opened-mouth, dumbfounded glare from her. His brother overhead her while standing behind her. He had come in again through the other entrance to the kitchen.

"You haven't heard a thing I said," she responded with hurt in her voice.

"Because she is a parasite woman with no scruples or shame who decided to live off the Indians, that's why. The way I see it, they deserve each other," his brother declared.

"Shut up, Mike!" Claudine shouted in frustration, wishing she could actually shut up her husband. She stood up from her chair and stood up against him until he humored her back to her senses.

Jeff's sister-in-law asked forgiveness for her husband, even though it was not necessary, since he knew his brother better than anyone except for his wife. While growing up, his brother and his crippled neighbor had competed for the affection of Claudine who Mike eventually married. Their rivalry had ended in a brawl. It was reason enough for him to heap his animosity on the cripple, virtually delighting in every accusation. "Your brother really thinks the only reason she did it was because she could live off the government like so many white people think Indians do. If that were true, don't you think she would have left by now? All he gets is disability and food stamps, because he's unemployable. Do you think there's anyone around here who would take care of him the way she does? No, not one living soul," Claudine raved in her anger as though the lady in question had been her own sister.

His brother slowly reappeared in the kitchen to get himself another refill of coffee. Obviously, it was an excuse to intrude on them again. He walked to the coffee maker and added more hot brew to warm his cup. Slowly, he measured and added two teaspoons of sugar. She looked up at him to see if he would put his foot in his mouth again. "Have you told him?" Mike smiled, asking his wife in a melodious overtone, and Claudine sighed, turning her head away in submission. "I guess you haven't," Mike continued. "Well, the doctors believe he can be rehabilitated, but he won't make the effort. I say she is telling him not to do it, so they can continue to collect disability."

Jeff had to admit there was a mean streak in his brother. He was taking advantage of his wife. He was treating her like many of the little girls with whom they used to play in grade school. He knew his brother meant no harm, but in those days the teachers had intervened on behalf of the little girls whenever they could no longer endure him pulling their hair and such. Claudine had no one. Mike's wife was about to explode anytime now, and he suspected his brother was coming to this realization also, and would stop his harassing immediately. Mike and his wife opposed each other in a silent clinch, eyeball to eyeball, until Mike retreated just as Jeff thought he would. Quickly, Mike defused his wife's anger and their confrontration dissipated. After she regained her congeniality, Claudine offered him another cup of coffee, and he accepted it. Meanwhile, Mike returned to his magazine and television. "You must think I'm some kind of witch," Jeff," his sister-in-law confessed embarrassingly about her passionate stand.

"No, that's not true. I thought you did very well," Jeff encouraged her. "I know how Mike is. I grew up with him. When you married him and took him out of the house, we all said never again. He used to tease me to tears sometimes."

"Well, you know how I feel then. I love Mike and always will, even though he gets me so worked up sometimes. So have you visited them?" she asked.

"I'm just too afraid to. My sister has asked me the same thing. You know, we live right next door to them. I've been spying on them through the back door," he confessed.

"Why haven't you?" she asked him insistently.

"I have never told anyone this before, but I gave him a couple of dollars that morning he was hit in the head at the bootleggers," Jeff confessed, and it astonished Claudine.

"Oh, you poor guy," she immediately symphathized. "You must be feeling really awful. But you shouldn't blame yourself for what happened. It was an accident. You must believe that."

"Mike told me that the other day his wife has chased off anyone who has tried to visit him at their house. People are afraid to come by now. He has probably told her I was the one who gave him the money. She probably blames me and would shoot me if I were to set foot in their yard."

"She would not shoot you, believe me," she admonished. "I know her. It's all the drunks she has chased off. You're not a drunk, Jeff. You are probably one of the best friends he ever had."

"But I gave him the money," he insisted. "If I hadn't, he wouldn't have been anywhere near that place that morning."

Jeff's brother reappeared and sat down with them at the table, and it terminated their discussion. This time his brother appeared without any traces of his former antagonisms or callousness. "Well, brother," he said to him and then put his hand on his shoulder, "I'm going into town to get that beer I said I didn't have earlier. Want to come along? You can't sit here and talk to my wife all day long. She won't get anything done, if you do. I want to take you into town and show you off to some of my friends and tell what a professional bowler you are. What do you say?

"Sure, why not, I'm ready to go," he agreed, and turning to his sister-in-law, he said, "Thanks for the talk, it has helped. I'll let you know how it turns out."

Jeff parted with his sister-in-law with a happy, satisfied grin on her face. She had performed her good deed for the day, and now he had to go and do his. In the truck, Jeff told his brother he would not be going to town with him and asked him to drop him off at his neighbor's house instead. His brother only replied with an indistinguishable grunt. He realized he forgot his loan papers, but Jeff decided not to go after them just now. The loan papers could always keep for another day, but the weight he carried for so long was heavier than his 16-pound bowling ball. His personal bank account was about empty. But Jeff was more concerned about another type of account, which he should have balanced years ago. He was now ready to stop by an old friend's house to make another type of deposit.

His need to sit down and talk with a forgotten friend excited Jeff, and while it still urged him, he needed to act on its impulses, or else it may take another five years before the courage to deal with it would come again. Already the whole idea of it felt more comfortable, something he would have thought impossible just minutes earlier. It was going to turn out to be a better day than he had expected, and he smiled at his brother. The smile baffled Mike, and it irritated him, as though his brother was withholding some kind of deep secret from him. If it had been a secret, or whatever, that was no longer what it was. It was out there in the open for him to act on now. He wanted to explain it to his brother, but he would not listen. So when Mike stopped at his neighbor's house to let him off, he did not say anything. He just thanked his brother for the loan and waved to him as he drove away.

The Snake of Light

by Irvin Morris

Set on a bed of ash and embers, the pile of cedar kindling smoldered thickly before igniting finally into tiny flames that grew quickly, building up steadily in power and resonance until the fire leapt up the stovepipe with a hollow roar. Slowly it subsided, quieting in a while to a steady crackle that could barely be heard through the iron walls of the stove. Nearby, a kerosene lamp burned dimly atop a small, square table draped with a worn and faded oilcloth. A moth fluttered around the lamp, trying to reach the glowing flame inside, but it was repulsed again and again by the hot chimney glass. Scorched, it whirled away and careened erratically about the room. In time, it dropped onto the tabletop where it whirred in wild circles.

The room was small and octagonal and the lamplight scarcely illuminated it, reflecting off the log walls and patched mud chink with a dull, bronze-orange glow. Along one section of the wall a narrow bed sagged under a tattered quilt, next to a stack of dented suitcases and cardboard boxes covered with a drab olive towel. An old floursack served as a curtain for the sole window. Outside, the wind rose up, curling streamers of smoke away from the hogan and into the gathering darkness. Aside from the whir of moth wings and the subdued crackle of the fire, the room was empty of sound and motion.

Presently, however, there was a noise at the door. The doorknob turned and the door swung open. An elderly woman entered. She was laden with an armload of wood and her movements were slow. But it was more than just the weight of wood that slowed her. She was old and there were things on her mind. She dropped the wood into the woodbox by the door and rubbed her back. This kind of thing was getting to be too much for her, but who would do these things for her, she wondered. She sighed deeply and glanced across the room to a familiar object propped amid the clutter of her things on the towel covering the suitcases and boxes, a hand-tinted photograph in a silver frame. It was a picture of a young man.

In the eyes of the old woman, the picture moved; the dark eyes shone and a shy smile creased the corners of his mouth ever so slightly. But that was impossible. It was an illusion, and she knew it. He was gone, vanished, from her world as if he had never existed at all. "Shee'awée'," she murmured. She had always thought of him as her baby.

121

The dark night was one rendering of reality, the thoughts pre-occupying the old woman, another. In a span of years it had become, for her, a salve for the deep ache of his absence and the stark silence she had to endure day after day. Now and then she stirred from her thoughts to lay more wood on the fire, or to sip coffee from a blue, enamelware cup.

In time, a second moth emerged from the shadows and flew circles around the lamp. But she did not see it. The moth itself was insignificant, a shadow, but the incessant whir of its beating wings sparked the memory of a certain voice in her mind. Without thinking, she mouthed a single, silent word — Ashkii. The word was a name, and the name was a portal into her thoughts. Her mind had left the stark silence of the house and slipped seamlessly into another, more amicable reality.

She was a younger woman suddenly, a capable and imposing figure. "Áshkii!" She yelled from under the arbor. He was playing on the bank of a small wash nearby and pretended not to hear. She knew, though, that he'd heard and would come soon enough. His stomach will remind him of the stew that's simmering on the fire and the fry bread that I'm making, she thought, and laughed softly to herself. He would wolf it down and ask for more.

They were alone, the woman and boy. Both her man and her only child, a daughter, had gone on years before. The boy was her grandson and sole heir. At times his mere existence was such a medicine to her that she would wonder what it might have been like without him. But his presence was also a constant reminder of the circumstances surrounding her daughter's death. It hardly seemed possible, sometimes, that ten years had passed since that cold spring morning when he was born — and her daughter had died. He didn't know that the old lady had pulled him from her daughter's body when it finally ceased to struggle, and that she had been afraid he was dead, too, until he screamed. After that, she had been fiercely determined that he should live.

Sometimes, when he struck a certain pose, or said things in a certain way, the resemblance was so unnerving that her throat would tighten. But then, he had other features too and inevitably she would think bitterly about the unknown swain who was his father. "Ma'iini'!" She would mutter. She hated the coyote who had tricked her daughter.

The years had slipped by quickly, so quickly that just the summer before she had been astounded to realize one day that he stood nearly as tall as she. Looking back, she saw that their lives had been like the land around them, the days melting into years like the hills and washes receded into oneness with the vast desert landscape. She kept busy at her loom while he went out after the sheep each day, into the wide valley in search of pastures for the sheep and what adventures a young boy's imagination might create out of the hot sands and long hours of solitude. She made jerky and parched corn for him to take along and taught him to find water in the thick flesh of roots and cactuses.

One day, a strange cloud of dust appeared on the horizon at the far edge of the valley. Instinctively, the old woman sensed that something was going to happen. The dust cloud looked to her like a whirlwind. Whirlwinds were forces that could disrupt a person's harmony with the land. Something that powerful had the ability to lay lifepaths askew. She watched it descend into the valley and felt her scalp prickle. It was coming across the valley, toward her home.

It moved slowly, awkwardly, making its way laboriously around clumps of rabbitbrush and greasewood anchored in high dunes. In the hot, still air of the valley the dust rose sluggishly and hung suspended in the shimmer of heat waves. She saw it was attached to the earth with a dark object; far off and small, it resembled a black ant, but as it came closer, she saw it was a dark truck. Her heart quailed. Bilagáanaas. Bilagáanaas were said to be taking children from their homes to keep in their schools. She told him to run quickly into the hills with the small sack of jerky she pressed into his hand, and stay there until they had gone back across the valley. He shot her a wide-eyed look, and she felt a small wash of relief swirl within her, but then she saw his eyes fix on the approaching machine. In that instant, the consequences of the truck's appearance hit her. She felt a balance shift, something in the turn of events that threw their world off kilter. She wanted, somehow, to show him that the creeping truck was dangerous, but she didn't know how. Instead, she could only motion to him urgently and watch as he turned slowly and walked away.

It disturbed her that he was intrigued with the very thing she feared most — the alien world of the whiteman. Unwittingly, her hands curled themselves into fists. A swell of emotion rose inexorably within her and threatened the thin cage of her chest. They had, in a way, captured him already. With that understanding, she watched the approaching truck with fear, then hate, in her eyes. She might have felt better if the dog had stayed to challenge the machine, but it had followed the boy and she had to face the coming encounter alone. She took her place under the arbor and watched the machine crawl across the valley.

After a long time, the truck rolled to a stop a short distance from her home. She did not stir. She stared at the men as they climbed down from the truck. They were sweating profusely and perspiration glistened on the bald head of the taller one. They approached her cautiously as if they sensed hostility boiling within her, but they approached nevertheless and stood before her. She sat still, looking past them to the heat waves shimmering in the valley. She did not acknowledge their presence until the tall one cleared his throat. She looked up then and directed a cold stare into his blue eyes. He flinched and looked away. "Yá'át'ééh," he said, greeting her in her own language. She was not surprised, and ignored his proffered hand.

"'Aoo'." She acknowledged their presence mechanically.

She did not invite them into the arbor, and they stood shifting from one foot to the other in the hot sun. They squinted in the brilliant sunlight and the short one shaded his eyes with a soft, pink hand. Sitting in the deep shade of the arbor — like an animal poised defensively in its lair — she could see them better than they could see her.

While the tall one talked, the short one surveyed her home. His eyes narrowed at the sight of her old cribbed-log hogan, juniper-post corral and makeshift arbor. The tall one's command of the Navajo language was poor, and his voice boomed at her as if from across a broad chasm, but she understood anyway; they had come to take her grandson. It is the law, the tall one said. If her grandson did not go with them now, they would notify the Bureau Police. "You don't want to get into trouble with them, do you?" he asked her, drawing himself up to his full height. "No," she said, she wanted no trouble with them. She was an old woman. But if she had been younger it would have been different; she would have wrestled the lot of them to the ground. They shot startled glances at each other.

She glared at them steadily, and they kept their eyes averted to the tangle of brush and boughs covering the arbor. "He is all I have," she told them. "He is my arms and legs now that age is beginning to weigh heavily upon my limbs. They could understand that, couldn't they? Didn't they have children, too?" But they persisted.

The sun blazed relentlessly at the center of the cloudless sky. As it began to shift slowly from its apex, the heat intensified in the lowering angle and the land grew fiercely hot. The whitemen's shirts soaked through with sweat and they retreated into the scant shade cast by the hogan. From there, they continued their harangue. Finally, she tired of them and got up. No, she told them, they could not have him. You simply did not take children from their homes. More than that, she could teach him all the things he needed to know. She shook the sand from her skirt and walked past them into the hogan and closed the door. They knocked several times, but she remained motionless inside. After awhile, she heard the truck doors open and close. Then the engine roared to life. She listened to the truck moving away until she couldn't hear it anymore. Then she opened the door and leaned against the doorjamb. She clasped her thin arms around the ache in her chest and felt tears well up in her eyes. She knew they would not give up so easily.

124

She stirred from her thoughts and got up, the fire had died down and the stove was silent. She poked at the few remaining live embers with a piece of wood and blew on them gently. Gradually, the wood succumbed and burst into flame. Satisfied, she returned to her chair and sat down slowly. She put a piece of cold, rubbery tortilla into her mouth and chewed absently. Once more, her mind propelled her from the room into another reality.

It was spring. The sun was bright, warm, well back on its way from the vernal equinox, and a fine patina of green smudged the contours of the land. Her eyes kept vigil on the far horizon: soon he would come. Images of her grandson swam in her mind. He is now 12. They had kept him two winters already, returning him in the spring and reclaiming him in the fall. The brief months she had him with her provided her with a wealth of memories that sustained her when she was alone.

And hate sustained her. She hated them so much she clenched her teeth and looked to the hills to distract herself from the awful thing that was happening. "Ahalaanee'," she said, and felt a rush of love. She had wanted to take him and flee with him into the hills, but she understood the futility of that and had turned painfully away. Ironically, it had been two Navajo men, not Bilagáanaas, who had come for him one day. She had closed the door behind her and shut her eyes. She covered her ears to block out the sound of his screams as they dragged him away. After they had gone, she sat for a long time under the arbor, holding in her palm a bit of sand scooped up from his footprints.

The first time they brought him back, he jumped down from the still moving truck and ran to her, becoming suddenly shy at the last moment. But he hesitated only momentarily. Then he was himself again, talking and gesturing so fast that she had to laugh. He chattered about the things he'd seen and done and strange words rattled off his tongue, but she only half-heard them. She touched his face with her eyes and listened to the changes that had come into his voice. The strange words he used — and the new inflections on familiar words — were stark revelations of what they had already done to him. She realized with a sinking feeling that it would be like that from now on, that there might be no end to it.

As the years passed, she both feared and looked forward to his return from the Bilagaanaa's school. And she learned to anticipate — and ultimately accept — the changes he influenced in her world. It was only because he was her flesh and blood that she could overlook the growing rift between them that these changes represented. But it was a rift she could bridge with her memories, and she was determined that it would never grow too wide that she wouldn't reach him.

For most of the year she could only guess at what was happening to him, but when he returned the changes were always enough to cause her surprise. In as many years as there were fingers on her hand, she saw him grow from little boy to adolescent to young man. One year, he was a full head taller than she. The next time, his voice had changed. The following year he hesitated to go after the sheep — because, he said, it was woman's work. Finally one year he returned only to tell her he was leaving. War had broken out somewhere on the other side of the world, he told her, and he was going to help the Americans fight. She could do nothing except to prepare a medicine pouch for sacred pollen and protection amulets to ensure his safe return. He stayed a few days and then he was gone.

Her world descended into unrelenting silence.

Sometimes, as she followed the sheep, her mind wandered and she wouldn't be following the flock of old ewes out in the desert, but far off in a strange green land where her grandson fought for the whitemen who had taken him from her. Sometimes the loneliness was overwhelming and tears rolled down her cheeks. She lived in a strange world where everything revolved around her, but she was desperately alone. Eventually, she lost track of days, months, and sometimes, she thought, years. But even in the silence of her world, she clung to her memories. She drew on them like hardy desert plants draw on the deep, unseen waters of the desert for sustenance.

II

She hardly slept at all that night. He was coming home. The sheer weight of that fact made her toss and turn on her narrow bed until she had to get up. She went up sometime after midnight and looked up at the night sky. The constellations and countless bright stars twinkled like jewels, and the side hazy band of the Milky Way arched overhead like a luminescent spine. Somewhere off to the west, a lone coyote howled.

In the morning she went out again just as the sun broke through a thick bank of clouds hanging over the mountains to the east. Long shafts of sunlight probed the myriad folds and creases of the land around her. She breathed deeply of the invigorating morning air and felt so bouyant that she sang. The sheep bleated from the corral when they saw her, but there was something more important that she had to do. They would have to wait. She put on her seldom-worn velveteen blouse, the glossy red one with decorative buttons made out of shiny American coins. Then she combed back her hair and fastened it into a tight knot that pulled the skin of her face tautly across her cheekbones. It had been a long time since she'd last put on her silver and turquoise jewelry, but this was an occasion that called for nothing but the best. She sipped a cup of coffee while she waited for her neighbors who were taking her to the trading post. The trader had sent word that her grandson would be arriving on the supply truck.

She had just finished the coffee when she heard the distant whinny of a horse, and then just barely, the faint, lilting voice of a man singing. As the wagon drew nearer, there was the jingle of harnesses and the creak of wagon wheels. She went out and closed the door behind her. The neighbor's wife was sitting in the box of the wagon with her two daughters all wrapped in their finest shawls. This was an occasion for them too. She climbed into the back of the wagon and settled down for the long ride to the post.

They unharnessed the horses near the post and kindled a fire. Her neighbor left to join a group of other men gambling under the trees surrounding the post, while she and his wife set about fixing their noon meal. She secretly scrutinized the neighbor's daughters to see if either of them might make a good wife for her grandson. But she saw that they spent too much time idling and fussing with their clothes. They sat in the shade of the wagon while their mother made bread and cooked meat over the hot coals. No, she thought, they would not do.

They ate slowly, watching the comings and goings at the post. Shadows shriveled and evaporated in the heat as the sun took hold of the land. Heat waves danced above the dunes and plain, while overhead buzzards wheeled lazily in the rising thermals. In time, the time for the arrival of the supply truck drew near. She kept herself busy helping her neighbor's wife with this and that so they would not see how anxious she really was. Later, she visited with the people gathered under the long porch fronting the post, laughing and jesting with them good-naturedly. A feeling of expectation charged the air. Frequent glances were cast down the dirt road that wound out of the valley. Suddenly there was a shout; the truck had been sighted. She straightened her shawl and smoothed her skirt.

The truck pulled up to the post in a cloud of dust and some of the men rose to help the trader unload his supplies. They hefted boxes of tins, iron tools, bolts of bright cloth and numerous bundles — but they might as well have been old sheepskins. Where is he, she wondered, and then she saw him. He stepped down from the cab of the truck and stretched. He scanned the crowd casually, and toward the rear of the crowd, he saw her. She made her way through the crowd and quietly embraced him. He saw that her eyes brimmed with tears and he felt embarrassed. "Yá'át'ééh," he said, and gently grasped her hand. Then the neighbors stepped forward with hearty greetings and proffered hands. The two girls were suddenly coy. The people looked at him, at how the medals pinned to the front of his uniform glinted in the sun. He was tall and handsome and someone speculated — by his appearance — who his father might have been. The two girls tried to capture his attention with their finery and affected coyness. She had never been so happy in her life. He had come home at last.

A wild storm broke not long after they had started for home, and they were soaked. The horses bent to the wheels, but the road was muddy and sudden rivers of brown storm water blocked their way. The fine shawls bled their colors and the girls were bedraggled. Then just before they arrived at the hogan, the rain abated and a brilliant rainbow appeared in the mist under the immense grey belly of the stormcloud.

The lamp flickered wildly as a moth dropped down into the chimney of the lamp and burst into flame. Her breath caught in her throat as an image flashed in her mind. In slow motion, a fixture in khaki green metamophosed tortuously into a twisted mass. The moth beat frantically against the glass, but it was trapped hopelessly and burst into flame.

Several years after he left for the whiteman's war, a crew of men had marched across the valley, leaving behind a line of stakes to mark the path of a highway that would soon cut the valley in two. She saw the road as a further sign of the assault on her world. Like a deadly and efficient predator, the road soon began exacting a heavy toll on the life of the valley. The shells of innumerable insects and carcasses of animals soon littered the sides of the pavement. Only the scavengers found reason to rejoice, or so she imagined as she watched the unremitting carnage. In her mind's eye, the universe was gripped in chaos.

The morning after he returned, he got up before daybreak. She heard him stir the ashes through the grate inside the stove. Soon, there was the familiar roar of the fire rising up the stovepipe.

As she peeled potatoes, she noticed that he was ill at ease. He fidgeted, clasping and unclasping his hands. He stared listlessly into space and nodded vaguely at things she said, and she wondered what it was that beckoned so strongly. The potatoes spattered and sizzled as she dumped them into the hot grease. He looked at her then, his attention focused entirely on her seemingly for the first time since he'd been back. He saw an old woman, brown as a pinon nut and weathered like an old tree. She was his grandmother and she had raised him, but something had changed and he felt as if he were looking at her through someone else's eyes.

He had been away for many years and he'd seen and done many things. He had experienced firsthand the whiteman's world, seen their marvelous inventions and the awesome power of their weapons. He had seen their bustling cities and tasted of their food and their women, sailed around the earth and seen it from 30,000 feet up. But he had learned, too, of his inferior place in that world, and it was with that experience that he looked at her now, as a whiteman might look at an old Indian woman, through a barrier of words and things. He saw a wizened squaw frying potatoes for breakfast in an old ramshackle hogan out in the middle of nowhere.

They ate in silence and he watched her, acutely aware of the way she ate. He saw that she had only a few teeth left and had trouble eating. Her face was deeply wrinkled and wisps of grey hair stuck in the air like antennae. He was surprised that he could distance himself like that and look at her so coldly, so flatly.

She wiped off the dishes carefully, put them away after they'd finished eating, and sat down. She wanted to talk to him about a few things now that he was back, about how tradition dictated certain things: namely, taking a wife and settling down. Iina — life — was the thing. He listened to her low voice and remembered when he could hear her yell from a long ways off. The new voice made him feel cheated. It was a fragile, hollowed-out shell of what had once been. A sharp undercurrent of loss cut at him and he felt something give way, some fundamental support collapse into the tumult of emotion. He felt the change so intensely that he wanted to leave the room.

At school all they had talked about was becoming something, a carpenter, plumber, electrician — anything, as long as it fit in with design. But now here she was, sounding like he was back for good. Here she was making plans and telling him things that didn't matter, that couldn't possibly fit in with what he'd learned to want. As he listened to her, he realized that he could not stay.

After a few days, he left with the excuse that he was going to the trading post, but he kept going until he found himself sitting at a dingy table inside a dark, bordertown bar. Through a haze of alcohol and cigarette smoke he caught a glimpse of himself in a bar mirror and flinched. He wondered what he was doing there, but he couldn't answer that so he just ordered another drink. He could not bring himself to go back to the old woman's place in this condition and face the disappointment in her eyes. He would wait, he decided, maybe tomorrow, maybe the next day. He didn't know.

The sudden appearance of her grandson, drunk at her door after two weeks absence startled and shocked her, but she bit back the hurt and hot tears long enough to leave the hogan. She sat down in the dirt under the arbor and listened to him moving around inside. She slumped with the grief, remembering the day long ago when she had sat there with a fistful of dirt scooped up from his footprints. She remembered her fervent prayer that he would return to her whole, unaffected by the influences of the whiteman's world. "Shee'awee'," she whispered, as she scooped up a fistful of dirt and let it sift through her fingers. An involuntary sob escaped from her lips.

Later, when she went back inside, he was snoring loudly on the cot. The smell of alcohol nauseated her, but she covered him with her quilt. She knew she would accept this change in him like she had accepted all the other changes he had wrought in her world. He was, after all, her flesh and blood.

III

The highway tops a hill before it winds past the bar. At certain times of day traffic flows along it so thick that it forms near solid lines. At dusk, and into the night, thousands of headlamps come on and fuse into long glittering strings of light that follow the rise and fall of the hills, skirting allotted lands and leaping over deep washes on steel bridges.

Not long after the highway had snaked through the valley, a square cinderblock building had appeared beside the road. It was a bar, and soon a ragtag queue of hollow-eyed men and women, distracted from their tasks and lives, haunted its periphery. He found himself frequently among their ranks, pressed up against the rough blocks like a cold fly on a wall.

Once, while sharing a bottle with someone on the hill behind the bar, a terrifying vision struck him. The stream of headlamps on the highway below coalesced into a shining, solid body — a snake made of light. He saw it coil, rear up and strike at him and he scuttled blindly backwards. "Hey, buddy!" His friend shook him, "Take it easy. Calm down, shi-buddy. You'll be okay." But even then his heart took a long time to slow down even a little. In his mind he saw the glittering snake with malefic, heat-seeking eyes turn to face him.

It was starkly cold, that winter night. His foot kept catching on things and he stumbled and tried to steady himself, but the earth whirled and spun. He collapsed in the tall grass and weeds lining the highway and pulled a bottle from his pants. He took a swallow, gagged, but kept it down. He rose to his feet unsteadily and looked to the crest of the hill to see if any cars were coming. He was bone-tired and sick and wanted only to go home. The old woman would let him in, he knew, even as she scolded him for being drunk again. He looked to the top of the hill once more. Nothing stirred in the night, and the sky was full of incredible beauty, countless stars that winked and glinted in the crystalline air.

He lurched awkwardly onto the highway, swaying with each step. His feet dragged and the earth reeled. His shoe caught on a crack in the pavement, and he went crashing. His face hit the pavement and a stream of blood spurted from his nose. He closed his eyes against the detonation of lights in his vision. He trembled uncontrollably as the ground spun and the darkness fell around him. He pressed his cheek against the warm pavement. He lay huddled on the highway, knees drawn up like a baby, and dimly became aware of a sound. What it was, or where it came from he didn't know. All he could make out was that it was growing. Strangely, he felt nothing — not cold, not fear, nothing at all. It was like he had become detached from his body.

The sound grew, sending dim vibrations through the chill air. Suddenly, a pair of headlights appeared at the top of the hill, and then another, and another. They grew into a long line of lights that descended sinuously down the hill. He opened his eyes and stared impassively as the snake with glittering eyes came inexorably toward him. At the last moment he closed his eyes. The night exploded into a maelstrom of light.

The driver of the first car saw nothing at first, then a dim shape on the road, but he could not stop. Like a silent scream, brakelights flared and bathed the night with a bloody red glow. The line of cars did not stop until several of them had passed over him. In the darkness and silence of the aftermath there was the sound of a woman sobbing, "We didn't see. We just didn't see."

The old woman shuddered and stirred from her thoughts. The room had grown cool and the stove was silent. She brushed her fingers against her cheeks to shoo away a moth that fluttered there, but finding tears instead, rubbed them between her fingertips. She got up slowly from her chair and blew out the lamp. She felt her way to her bed with her feet and sat down wearily. In the morning she would take the sheep out and follow them into the valley, moving from one clump of greasewood to another, seeking the scant shelter they offered from the chilling wind. The day after that would be no different. At last, she lay down and closed her eyes.

The Hot Desert Breeze: A Children's Story

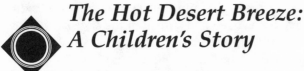

by Robert L. Perea

The people had lost much of their culture, many of their traditions, many of their stories. That's what the man had heard. But the spirit was still with them. Like the hot desert breeze. And that's what mattered most.

"It scares me, Bob," she said standing up and flicking on the lamp at the head of the bed. He looked up to the Winnie-the-Pooh on her pajamas.

"Turn off the light!" he yelled reaching over to touch the switch.

"It scares me, Bob," she repeated.

"There's nothing to be afraid of," he said covering her with a blanket. "The Man-in-the-Moon is outside."

"Oscar?" she asked.

"Oscar's sleeping in the garbage can, outside," he answered.

"Tell me a story, Bob," she said. "The one about the big giant."

"Go to sleep, Stacey," he told her. "It's way past your bed time. You should be asleep."

"Just one story, Bob," she asked again. "Just one story."

"O.K., just one story, but you better go to sleep after that."

"I promise, Bob."

"O.K."

"Once upon a time," he started, in a slow, soft, magical voice, "long, long, time ago there lived a little boy by the name of Jack. Jack lived in a little house with his mommy. One day Jack's mommy told Jack to go to the store to buy some food."

"His mommy didn't has no food," Stacey added.

"Right, Jack's mommy didn't has no food because that mean ol' giant had taken all their food."

"That giant's mean," Stacey said in a serious voice. "I hate that giant."

"Me, too," Bob said. "Anyway, Jack's mommy gave Jack some money to go to the store to buy some food. So Jack went to the store, but all the food in the store was gone. The giant had taken all their food, too! That mean ol' giant. The only thing the man at the store had was a handful of beans. When Jack got home, his mommy was real mad at him. 'You gave

132

away all our money for these beans!' she yelled at Jack. 'Go to your room right now and don't come out!' And she took the beans and threw them out the window. Poor Jack. He was real sad. He was crying because his mommy was mad at him and they didn't have no food to eat."

"Poor Jack," Stacey said in a sad voice.

"So Jack went into his little room and put on his little pajamas and went to sleep. He wasn't scared of the dark either."

"Anyway, all of a sudden in the middle of the night little Jack woke up. He heard a noise outside. He peeked out the window and saw a tree growing way up to the sky. So he got out of bed and put his little shoes, his little socks, his little pants, his little shirt, he put on all his clothes and climbed out the window. And he climbed that big tree. He climbed and climbed until he came to a big cloud."

"The Man-in-the-Moon, huh?" Stacey asked.

"He looked up and there was the Man-in-the-Moon looking at him. But he didn't get scared. He asked that Man-in-the-Moon where the giant was. And the Man-in-the-Moon told him. So he went looking for the giant's big house."

"The giant's big catho'," Stacey corrected.

"The giant's big castle," Bob said laughing. "The giant's big, big castle. Pretty soon little Jack came to a big door. He opened the door and peeked inside. He didn't see anything so he went inside where he saw another big door. He peeked inside that door and guess what he saw?"

"What?" asked Stacey afraid to ask, yet knowing the answer.

"He saw that big mean giant!" he said. He stopped and looked at Stacey in the dark and almost started to cry.

"That big mean giant was sleeping," Stacey said sensing Bob had momentarily stopped telling the story.

"Right, that big mean giant was sleeping," he continued. "And all around him was food. There was i'creams, 'ogurt, pop'orns, 'ritos, M & M's, bubble gums, 'tato chips. All kinds of food that mean ol' giant had taken from everybody. Plus Cokes and Peppers and Candy Dry and Lipes," he said choking back the tears.

"Why's Bob crying?" Stacey asked.

"It's a sad story," Bob said.

"The story's real sad," Stacey repeated.

Bob continued to tell the story. He got to the part where the beanstalk was swaying back and forth. Jack had just used his axe on it and the giant was hurriedly trying to climb down the beanstalk.

"Like this," Stacey said putting up her little chubby arm. She imitated the swaying of the beanstalk as it was about to fall. She moved her arm back and forth, back and forth, until . . .

"Poom!" she laughed as she dropped her arm imitating the crashing of the beanstalk to the ground. Bob finished the story.

"Tell me another," Stacey said.

"Go to sleep," he meekly insisted.

"I not tired," she said. "Tell me another story."

"Say, please," Bob said. She looked at him.

"Please, daddy," she said hugging him tightly. He started to cry again.

So he told her another story. In the middle of it she fell asleep. He couldn't sleep that night. He spent most of his time waking up, gazing at her and occasionally giving her a kiss on the cheek while she slept. He knew that shortly, he would never see her again.

*　　　*　　　*　　　*　　　*　　　.　*

"There's the catho'," the little girl yelled excitedly. "There's the giant's big catho'. I see it! I see it!" The hot sun pounded the old Torino as they drove west on the Maricopa Freeway. The miniature castle on the miniature golf course quickly faded from view.

"Is that mean ol' giant following us?" asked the man driving. The little girl gazed hard out the back window looking for the giant in case he was following them.

"He better not," the young boy, seated next to the little girl, said smiling at the man.

"Yeah, he better not," added the man.

"Oscar will get him," said the little girl.

"The giant will only get you if you're bad," said the boy.

"I been good!" the little girl quickly insisted.

"That's right, you have been real good," the man added.

"Did you behave yourself at Huggy Bear this morning?" asked the boy, referring to the day care center the little girl attended.

"I din't bite nobody, I din't pee-pee in my pants. I been good," the little girl proudly said.

They continued on the freeway heading for the amusement park.

"We're almost there," the man said as he slowed the Torino to exit the freeway.

"Are you tired, Stacey?" asked the man.

"I not tired," the little girl answered.

"Let me look into your eyes."

"I not tired!" the little girl insisted.

"Bob's just teasing," the man said softly.

They took the off-ramp to the amusement park.

"Where's Stacey's mom?" the young boy asked.

"I don't know, Garrick," the man said. "She's gone to California, I guess."

"My mommy's in Ca'fornia," the little girl said.

"She's in California," the man repeated.

"She's mean," the little boy said.

"My mommy's not mean!" argued the little girl. The little girl stared out the window of the Torino.

They passed over the Salt River on the way to the amusement park. El Rio Salado. They still couldn't see the lights of the park.

"The next time your mommy does that to you," Garrick said, "I'm gonna, 'Pow!', right in her . . ."

"My mommy's not mean," the little girl said.

"Id like to kick her fuckin' ass from here to California," thought the man, but he knew she'd like that.

"That giant is mean," the man said.

"That mean ol' giant," the little girl repeated.

"Your mommy drinks beer, but she's not mean," said the man.

"My mommy don't drink beer," argued the little girl," she drinks 'quila."

The little girl stared out the window, thoughts racing through her head.

She looked at the man, then the boy, and stared out the window of the Torino again.

"Pow!" said the young boy laughing, looking at the little girl.

"Pow," laughed the man, hesitating at first.

The little girl stared out the window again.

"Pow," she finally said, but holding it back.

"Pow," she repeated, laughing a little.

"Pow," she said again hitting her hand with her first.

"If your mommy tries to do anything more to you," the little boy said, "we're all gonna . . ."

"Pow! Pow! Pow!" screamed the little girl, hitting her hand with her fist.

As they pulled up to the amusement park there was total bedlam in the Torino. The man, the young boy, and the little girl were screaming, yelling, kicking into the air, slamming their hands with their fists, and laughing. They didn't even bother to look outside the car. They knew that mean ol' giant wouldn't dare follow them.

*   *   *   *   *   *

The apartment room reverberated with sounds of music. Funky disco, as it was called. Music to dance to. Music to sweat to.

135

The woman danced to music in perfect rhythm. Her two year old daughter wandered around aimlessly. The woman's girl friend danced, too. The girl friend's two boys jumped up and down laughing and playing.

The little daughter looked up at her mother. She grabbed her mother's leg.

"Stacey, not now," the woman said. "Mommy's dancing."

The little girl decided to play on a large rocking horse, but one of the boys wouldn't let her.

"Melody, Stacey's fighting again," said the woman's girl friend.

"Stacey, leave Danny alone!" the woman yelled at her daughter as she continued dancing.

"My horse," thought the little girl watching the little boy climb on her rocking horse. "My horse," she said. She went into her room and curled up in bed. She carefully folded her hair around her hand and began sucking her thumb.

A man knocked at the door, but realizing the loud music muffled his knock, entered the room.

"Hello, Melody," said the man. The woman turned the music down.

"There's some cokes and beer and wine in the 'frig," the woman said. "Help yourself." She turned the music back up and continued dancing. The man walked into the little girl's room.

"Stacey," he whispered. Immediately the little girl jumped out of bed and ran to him. He picked her up and hugged her tightly, carrying her to the kitchen where he grabbed a coke from the refrigerator. The man sat down in the corner with the coke.

The little girl walked over to the little boy on the rocking horse.

"My Bob," she said, proudly pointing to the man. The little boy heard her, but ignored her and kept on rocking. She went over to the other little boy and said the same thing. The other little boy ignored her, too.

The little girl started to approach her mother, but her mother was dancing so hard she decided not to. Finally, she went over to her mother's girl friend who was standing, sipping some wine from a glass, moving her head to the music.

"My Bob," the little girl said to her mother's girl friend, tapping her on the leg. The woman didn't even look down.

"My Bob! My Bob!" the little girl yelled above the music, frantically hitting the woman on the leg trying to get her attention. The woman finally looked down at the little girl.

"My Bob," the little girl said proudly, once again pointing to the man. The woman sneered at the little girl. The man immediately glared at the woman. The little girl ran back to the man and jumped into his arms, hugging him tightly.

The house was an old one, surrounded by the lush green woods, the Cayuga woods. The woods where arrow heads and ancient corn grinders could be found. Where sacred mounds could be found. Where the spirit of a people once lived. The farm family, a large one, was nervous. They had a new daughter. She was a pretty little girl. Three years old, lovely blond hair, dressed in a jogging outfit. The kind you see week-end runners wear, only here was a child's. A child's jogging outfit.

"This is your new mommy," said the aunt. The aunt who'd brought the little girl to the Cayuga woods. The little girl looked at her new mother again, then stared out the window of the farm house. My new mommy looks like my old mommy, the little girl thought. The little girl clung tightly to her aunt.

"Edward is anxious to leave," said the aunt. "Besides, Sis', I've done my job. She's all yours." The aunt pushed the little girl away and hurriedly left.

The little girl glanced at her new family, all the strange faces staring at her, then looked at the floor.

"Stacey, this is your new home," said the new mommy gently reaching to touch the little girl. The little girl wrapped her blond hair around her hand and shoved her thumb into her mouth.

"You shouldn't do that," the new mother said. "Don't suck your thumb."

"What's this?" asked one of the boys rummaging through the little girl's luggage.

"It's a picture book," said the new mother.

"Who's this strange man with Stacey?" asked the boy. "How come there's all these pictures of her with this strange man?"

"That's my daddy," the little girl said.

"That's not your daddy," the newe mother said. "He's just a friend of your mother's . . . I mean, he's just a friend."

"Bob's my daddy," the little girl insisted.

"His full name is Lazaro," the new mother said.

"He looks strange to me," the little boy said. "What is he?"

"He's Indian or Mexican or something like that," the new mother said.

"I read they have Pimas and Apaches over there," said one of the older boys. "I read about that in school."

"He still looks strange," the little boy said.

"She needs to be with her own kind," said the new mother.

"Bob's my daddy," the little girl said grabbing the picture book.

137

"I can't understand why a man would bother with a little girl who's not even his," the new mother said.

"Where's her real daddy?" asked the older boy.

"Nobody knows," answered the new mother.

"Bob's my real daddy," argued the little girl tightly clutching her picture book.

"He's your boy friend," laughed the boy. "You got a boy friend, you got a boy friend, you got a boy friend," he chanted.

The little girl viciously kicked the boy. The new mother quickly grabbed the little girl and shook her.

"Listen here, young lady!" the new mother yelled, "you're going to have to behave yourself if you're going to live here."

"The Big Bad Wolf's gonna get you," the little boy teased.

"Laddy, leave her alone," said the new mother.

That night the little girl kept waking up. Her dreams were scaring her. Where was her daddy, she thought. She knew she had to find him. So she climbed out of bed and carefully put her little jogging outfit and her little tennis shoes on. She made her way to the kitchen and opened the refrigerator. There she found an open can of pork and beans and grabbed it. Outside, in the darkness, she poured the beans all over the ground. Then she ran back inside. The Man-in-the-Moon watched her the whole time. She got back in bed and waited and watched. But nothing happened as she peered out the window. She couldn't understand why. Finally, she carefully wrapped her hair around her hand, put her thumb in her mouth, curled up, and went to sleep fully expecting the beanstalk to be there when she awoke.

The next morning her new mother was surprised to find the little girl asleep in her little jogging outfit and tennis shoes. Her tennis shoes were sticky with beans. After bathing the little girl, the new mother tried to dress her in jeans. The little girl refused to co-operate. The new mother finally got her dressed after much screaming, kicking, and crying.

"Laddy and Prissy," the new mother said, exhausted, to two of her children. "Take your new sister outside and keep an eye on her. I've got to shower and dress."

The two children watched their new sister as best they could. But when some horses caught their attention, the little girl snuck inside the farm house, grabbed her picture book, desperately ripped off all her clothes and ran. She ran like a child on fire tightly clutching her picture book. Terrified, she ran into the Cayuga woods crying and shaking until a neighbor found her.

After that, the story went around about the little girl running naked in the woods. Everyone thought it was funny. The little girl didn't think it was funny. Neither did the strange man. Neither did the Man-in-the-Moon. The living spirit that mattered most was still with them, and the spirit would not let the girl, the man, the people, the story, be laughed away and lost. That's what the man heard now.

The Wild Birds

by Mary Tallmountain

Summary: During World War I, Clem is stationed in the U.S. Army at Nulato, a remote Alaskan village. He and Mary Joe, an Indian/Russian woman, have two children, Lidwynne and Michael. Mary Joe develops tuberculosis and gives Lidwynne to the government doctor and his wife for adoption. The village council will not permit them to have Michael.

At war's end, Clem is transferred; Lidwynne and her second parents go Outside; and for 50 years she and Clem are parted. He hears that she is dead. She hears that he is retired in Phoenix but her letters are not answered. Years pass, and she gives up the search. In 1977 during a visit she finds Clem, living in Sunnyslope with 15 wild birds in cages. She moves to Phoenix to live. The 85-year-old Clem is pondering his astonishing new situation.

Clem felt better. He and Lidwynne had aired a few old grudges. Settled 'em, too. He knew it was hard for a girl to get under the hide of an old crocodile like him, when they'd been strangers for years. But he didn't think, by God, that she realized how long he'd been a loner. Stuck in his ways. Feisty and radical, he thought, too. Loner or not, he'd managed to apologize to his daughter for butting into her business. How lucky he was to get her back now, better'n 50 years later. His damnfool Air Force buddies had put it on the Morse Code grapevine years ago that she'd married and died in Nova Scotia. But now he'd found that she was alive, and that her whole life was a mystery, to him. She'd been alone since her husband died; he thought she'd said that was over 30 years ago, but Clem knew his dates were fuzzy. Smart and pretty like her, she must've had somebody, sometime. His damned old jealousy had started simmering. He shivered, recalling how he'd pestered and nagged her with questions, till finally she ignored him completely. But he kept on, making ironic remarks now. Fed up with these bombardier tactics, she yelled at him. He had no gumption. If he had any at all he'd quit prying into her biz. Furthermore, if he didn't quit it, she downright laid it down. She'd get out of his life.

Damnit, this had been their first fuss. He'd butted into her business with his big yapp. "Bet your boots I won't do that again and I told her so like a gentleman," he mused aloud.

One reason he was crazy about his girl Lid, she was an awful lot like Becky, her grandmother. Spittin' image. Even sounded like her talking.

To listen to her, it was like they'd been transplanted right into Mother's country kitchen in Hoptown, California, in the 1890s. Their voices were exactly alike to the last drawling southern lilt. Well, he was his mother's boy, all right, Clem thought, and the image of Becky floated over the years into his mind, her pale skin faintly filmed with sweat, sunbleached hair blowing across the silvery pins that dotted it. The unfathomable look in her eyes; what did it mean? He shivered, thought, Mother's a-walkin' on my grave, and chuckled. What the hell was I thinkin', he wondered. Oh, yes, Becky. Mother. He said aloud, "Mother, Muh-th-err," purring out the words as long and slow as he could, the way his mind had forever said it, in a tender tone like a warm note on his fiddle.

Sure, see, he'd been around Mother so close he'd taken on himself a lot of her ways. Gentle, quiet-like. Later in the army, he'd lost most of it. Little old Clemmie'd had to get tough, for a tough army. He'd toughened up plenty in Alaska. The Indians had taken him in tow when they saw how savvy he was about guns and hunting. They'd got real friendly after a year or two. He'd learned some of their ways by then, and they took him hunting and fishing, taught him their wrestling holds, kicking tricks, gambling games. Yep, Clem showed them he was no weakling. But on the other hand, he wasn't mean. There was no way he'd ever lose all of that kind of gentleness he'd got from Becky. It was the half of him that was her.

"Yep," he said. "Becky." What had he been thinking? Had he taken a little snooze again? "Yep," he repeated. Oh, now he knew. He'd been thinking about Becky and Lid, the two of them sort of melting together in his skull till they were like one woman. He'd have to try to please the girl more. He'd get his woozy old head to workin' better, even if it seemed like, sometimes, he didn't know what was goin' on at all, and things got sort of foggy like just now. He squared the angles of his thin shoulder bones. He'd change his cantankerous ways. Seeing himself in her eyes, he thought he must've been a shock to her. Some of his manners . . . he tried to change his eating habits. Alone so many years like this . . . It was good her cooking meals regularly. When he wasn't too fuzzy he'd wash up like he used to for Becky. Sometimes he'd forget detergent, or leave stuff in the sink. Putting dishes away was the worst. By himself he never put them away in the same places. It didn't matter then.

It had turned different. Maybe he was confused, he thought. Lid was sorting away, and throwing out all sorts of things. She had noticed the house was full of roaches and that mice had chewed on every stitch he owned, not that there were many items any more; he'd been used to dressing in uniform all his life. No wonder since he retired, he'd been like Becky used to say, just a ragtag and bobtail. But he was going to change

. . . Lid said all those sacks of grain stacked away for his 15 birds attracted varmints and such. She aimed to clean up the place so's she could move from the motel and live in the house. Every time he thought about that, he busted out whistling. Lid would be here in the house with him!

He shook himself out of a little doze. His first thought was: It will sure be easier on her being right here. His second thought was: That damned irrigation business. His mind seized and shook this thought like a terrier with a bone. It was too much for her, every day. Why hadn't anybody told him he'd have to do an irrigation every day. Had Doc told him and he'd forgotten, that time he'd had the colostomy? He tended to get flustered when there were different happenings. When he'd got sick and Lid took him to the hospital, she'd found out how to irrigate, and now she was helping him with it. It made that much more work for her. She didn't seem to mind, even offered to help care for the birds! But he just couldn't lay that on her.

He still had three birds. Only these three out of the 15 beautiful wild birds, all the others gone in a single night. A strange, strange happening. His suspicions circled and returned to Dack, his half-crippled neighbor. Dack was only a lot and a half away — nobody else had been here. Clem had slept like a rock and when he got up, Dack had already come over and was wiping his eyes and pointing to the cages, the little dead fellows just dark piles. Clem didn't know how he'd managed to get through the next few days. All his birds dead. He realized he'd been caring for them 16 hours a day.

Lid had arrived in Phoenix the next day from Frisco to stay with him. A week later he'd gotten so sick she'd had to put him in the hospital. After the doctor said he'd had too much stress and shock, because of the abrupt reunion with Lid and the loss of so many birds, he rested a few days and Lid took him home. Then he started forgetting things. Nothing had mattered to him before she came, nothing but those birds. The work had taken so much out of him there was nothing left. No reminders of his empty life, even. How much he'd wanted to have his daughter here, how he'd begged her in his letters. Now she was so close, just across the street, and he didn't know what was the matter with his head. It was so funny, so damned foggy. He forgot to tell her how he enjoyed life now, and God, he even forgot sometimes that she was here!

He wondered what he could do. His chin bobbed against his ravelly collar. A warm silence settled in the room, broken only by the soft rustles of the three sleeping birds.

Startled awake, Clem saw by the darkening evening that it was later than his usual bedtime. He squinted at the clock. Nine. I wonder how long I've sat here, he thought. Faint light came in under the ragged windowblind. The air was tense, sticky. The birds smelled damp and yeasty.

142

How many nights I've sat here with them, snoozed off, woke up and saw them hunched asleep in the cages. They don't know what's going to happen. His mind started a monotone: I have to do it. Lid will leave me if I don't do it. I'll be all alone.

He straightened. "Now I'll go do it," he said, as if in answer to another voice. He stumbled, going to Bobo's cage. When he laid his hand on it, Bobo raised his long, scissorlike beak. It's the last time I'll see you look up at me, old fellow, Clem thought. Carefully lifting the cage, he shuffled out the door. It was dark on the porch but he found the screen-door handle. Street light drifted down into the yard. Again he tripped, stepping over to the mulberry trees where the leaves seemed to be quivering. His hand shook, unfastening the cage.

The mockingbird hopped up and down. One black, shining eye pierced the shadows. Clem tapped the side of the cage. "Go to it, old Bobo." His voice shook. Bobo gathered himself and swelled up fat as an apple. With a curious "phwet," he ran to the door of his cage and stared up into the trees. He flicked an eye back at Clem. Five or six steps took him out of the cage. He leaned forward, wings apart, heavy body straining up. Clem trembled. When he opened his eyes, Bobo was gone. Clem left the cage open and went back inside.

Talking to Stringy, Clem thought the linnet looked smaller and darker than usual. Switching on the overhead, he thought, "I didn't realize it was dark in here." The bird was still, except for his darting head. Clem said, "You been here 15 years, huh?" The brown head dipped quickly, and Clem thought: "They claim birds don't understand what you say."

Under the mulberry he set Stringy's cage alongside the other. He opened the door, thinking, he's nervous and jumpy, so different than big fat rascal Bobo. I'll let him take his time. But Stringy instantly ran for the open door. Out clear and away, he took to the air with one short piping call. Clem watched him this time. The bird flew in a long curve upward, wings smoothly fluttering across the yard to the palo verde tree next to Dack's back porch. Up there, he'll be safe, Clem thought.

His teeth clicked, but it wasn't cold tonight, it was warm. Now, Sophia, my little crippled sparrow. She wasn't like that when I got her. No, that was Dack's damn doings. He still heard Sophia's screams when Dack's big hand had nearly crushed her. She'd caught a claw as Dack had tried to get her out of the cage. Ten, 12 years ago, Clem thought. Getting hard to remember. He'd often thought there was something crazy wrong with Dack. His face had gone black as a thunderhead and when the tiny claw wouldn't come loose Dack squeezed her and squeezed her. Sophia shrieked once, and Clem ran forward, yelling to Dack to stop. Dack's face

143

twisted. Clem struck hard at his shoulder. Solphia dropped out of Dack's hand with her feet clenched to her body.

Clem's face felt cold now, as he held the cage and watched her lying in the corner. From that day of terror on, she had hauled herself around the cage by her beak. Her legs had stayed bent up to her breast. He had to feed her with eyedroppers. At last he saw she'd never walk again. So he took extra pains, more than he took with the others. When her claws got long, he trimmed them and cut away the matted excrement. It was the least he could do.

Once again, Clem thought: It was my fault, letting Dack care for the birds. I never did, again. Once in a while he'd cover the cages. He could never remember what he'd screamed that day, but Dack had left and stayed away a long time. When he slunk back, he was on the mooch as usual, and Clem let him have a few bucks to tide him over. He never offered to touch the birds. Neither of them ever mentioned the happening, and it was a dark shadow across their old friendship.

With just the three birds left, Clem kept Sophia's cage immaculate. He speculated: should I have put her out of pain a long time ago? I'd got into a habit, I guess. People brought me fallen birds, hurt birds. Lid doesn't understand how much good I've done. My own daughter. You can't cage wild birds, she says. Heal them and let them fly. She gets that from her Indian mother. Taking care of those little helpless things that needed me was — maybe some way I felt important, like somebody useful. They were there, alive, waiting for me —

His mind whirled with disjointed words. A stream of energy passed through his frail frame. In the kitchen he poured a dishpan full of water. Too cold, he thought, and ran more from the hot water tap. "That's better," he said.

Approaching Sophia, he thought her look was even more trusting than usual. She pecked softly at his gnarled thumb. He drew her gently out. Her sticklike legs jutted askew. Crazy Dack's strong piano-playing hand, Clem thought.

Standing with his eyes shut tight, he pressed her head quickly under the water. Through his palm he felt her flapping and then trembling, felt the shivers fade, and finally stop. She looked all right, there under the water, one eye open and dark; Clem stroked the drops of water down along her lightly oiled feathers and knew in his own body the sadness of hers. He wrapped her in a sandwich bag, sealed its plastic seam. It took only an instant to lay her under the mulberry. He left the two empty cages and went in.

There, he thought. It's done. The wild birds are gone. Sitting in the tattered chair, he leaned against its arm and put his face down into his knotted hands.

BIA Boarding School #39
by Cynthia Wilson

Three of the third grade boys had head lice and the federal policy for reservation schools required that the teacher inspect daily and send notes back to the dorm. Shave them all bald, Miss Morris wrote in her perfectly even-spaced, upright printing. Then she folded the canary yellow notepaper with two folds like an official letter from the Government Office before she used her orange handled scissors to cut it into thin confetti strips. She could either make a bulletin board zinnia or pass the strips out as bookmarks. I'll decide later she thought. In the front of the classroom behind her blond oak desk, she readjusted her bra like a suit of armor and hated the identical, dark faces she saw. Miss Morris stood up next to a red construction paper balloon with the magic marker message, "Spelling is Fun!!!"

"Please get out your reading books to read the story entitled, 'The Milkman and His Friends' on pages 17 through 25. Do not whisper; this is silent reading time." She had trained this class in only six weeks, only half as long as the last two years classes. She was a pro now. This group obeyed the classroom rules completely, but she often got annoyed anyway. During silent reading she got edgy because the class fell to a deep and regular breathing, a sound reminiscent of the waves on the Hudson or the summer droning of insects on the East Coast. The sound tangled up New Jersey and Arizona in her mind. Here they have the beach with no water, she thought. She deserved a better school than this. "Anya Inez, put a pencil between your teeth. This is *silent* reading."

Miss Morris took a new ruler from the supply closet and called Jesus, Barney, and George to her desk for judgment. "Turn around. Face your backs to me," she said. She used the stick to lift a clump of the unwashed hair. The nits were sliding down the strands like counters on a Chinese abacus. What do lice eat she thought. She imagined George's brain infected with pus. They slid down the hair and onto his eyelashes when he tries to hide his face from me. Then they eat all his lashes and through the jelly of his eye. It is simple natural history; the strong will live off the weak. She sent the boys away after she reminded them to wash every night with the stinky soap the housemothers gave them. What did they call it? Bah-hock-dey, or something like that, in Papago.

In college, if only she hadn't heard how Hitler had admired the Americans for what they did to the Indians. She had imagined herself dressed in icy white, striding through villages, beloved. A female Schweitzer but svelte. With a peach-colored sunburn on her cheeks. A selfless woman. If only she wasn't here.

Back home third graders knew how to read a clock, could paint real-looking houses and buildings, and came to school clean. None of them would whisper a quiet, snakey language behind her back. The desert was ugly, no matter what *Arizona Highways* said. She could never find the picturesque sights the same as what was shown in the magazine in full romantic color. Everything was burnt weeds or tannish rock with almost orange lines running through it. It was like living in one of those brown-yellow, old-timey photographs of some miserable, plague-riddled place. Maybe the government had done secret tests out here, just like in New Mexico. The children here were strange, and the people were too silent; they must be dying out. Even the moon would be a sweeter place than this. You could have cities, and everyone could keep busy instead of losing their minds. The clock above Miss Morris' head shivered at two minutes until the hour while the class sighed and almost fell asleep. Miss Morris imagined she was coming out of the subway in Hoboken where you could see a green and red Coca-cola sign, and you could walk four short blocks to get great clams-on-the-half-shell or linguini, and you could think of Frank Sinatra growing up there. In the cities, there is always something to see or do or find out about. Things don't stagnate. You couldn't be too disturbed about anything because you are moving too fast.

After school everyday at 4:15, Miss Morris became Ruth and she walked home with her best friend, Abigail Zimmerman, the first grade teacher. Briskly, taking the shortest path between two points, they moved from the old buildings in the direction of the new cafeteria toward their houses. Together, they decided it smelled like the fatty, gray meat the dinner menu pretended was ham steak. It was dog food, Ruth thought.

Abby was laughing. It was Friday and the smell struck her as funny. "Poor kids, they never know what's what at dinner. At least in their folks' day they'd get fish on Fridays."

Ruth didn't think at all of the smell if she could help it, and she held her breath as she emptied her shoes of the dust from the schoolyard. She didn't lean on the fence post beside her because it was electrified, part of Sing-Sing's security. Abby had made up that name for the teachers' compound. It looked like a luxury prison with six evenly spaced two-story ranch style homes at the end of two paved cul-de-sacs. It was a necessity to get anyone out to this wilderness to teach. You needed a regular house with extras to survive. As Ruth looked at her own house, she thought

146

the federal jobs, on the whole, were decent enough. Or at least they brought some places out of the primitive ages, but some of the people who worked them sure missed the boat.

Speculation was the girls only regular after-work activity while at Sing-Sing, and Louise Martin was their favorite subject. Louise was 51 years old and taught all of her 18 BIA years at #39. The girls thought of her as a museum piece, something famous in the BIA annals as "Old-Stick-In-The-Mud." Or rather as Ruth said, "Stuck-in-the-Sand." Old Stuck had only two more years till retirement, and the girls were envious. However, they knew Louise wouldn't go back to civilization even then. She chainsmoked happily in the teacher's lounge and dressed like a cowboy (not at all like the role model the Administration wanted). You'd think the Indian men would hate her because she was so brassy and blunt, but she was engaged to Joe Oro who was half Indian and known as a good man. Imagine, at her age.

She'll never get out of here, Ruth often thought. If you made the 20 years in the BIA, the retirement could set you up. But Ruth was stuck here till her fifth year promotion or transfer would come up, and the closest Indians to New Jersey were in Wisconsin. Ruth had heard that up there they fired guns and had stand-offs with police over hunting or fishing or something dumb like that. The Bean People here at least knew enough not to get in trouble with the law. They had named themselves pretty well, come to think of it. Brown and slow and ordinary — the Bean People in a can nobody wanted. You couldn't even sell the land because nothing was opening up here. There are no developers because there's no progress.

Every Monday, Wednesday, and Friday, the girls ate dinner together at each other's house. But tonight the girls decided impulsively to drive the 50 miles into Casa Grande and go to the Cleaver Club for steak. After putting her feet up for a little while, Ruth had only five minutes to change from her lilac pantsuit to the smart, black wrap-around dress that she made from Simplicity 2133. After she squeezed her legs into an unstretched pair of black pantyhose, she could hear the nylon slide as one thigh grazed the other as she walked to the bathroom. She pulled her hair back severely from her face into a smooth ponytail. Above average, she thought. Approachable. Ruth had volunteered her sedan because it had a deep spare tire well in the trunk and two bottles of bourbon could fit easily. It had to be undetectable. They smuggled the booze home because the reservation was dry, and if one of the Indian Sheriffs stopped you at night, they would always look for liquor. The girls had never gotten stopped, but it was like living in one of those countries where the government agents would bust down your door and take you away.

At the Cleaver parking lot, Ruth recognized Louise's jeep immediately.

"Should we stay or should we go?" Abby asked. "You never know who the hell will be with her."

Inside, the girls found no one with Louise and the only polite thing to do was to ask her to join them for a drink. In a small corner booth, the three sat together as tightly as sisters and as if they were conspiring. Ruth bent over to run the heel of her dress pumps away from the tender spot on her heel. From this angle she could see closer into Louise's face, and she concentrated on the creases around Louise's mouth which stretched and relaxed like rubber bands. Ruth knew that Louise had been pretty at one time, but she couldn't quite visualize the transformation. People often told Ruth that she had a beautiful face, if only . . . Ruth felt that if she could be as thin as Louise, she would be perfect.

As usual, Louise asked if they'd learned anything new. The girls thought that she must ask her sixth grade class the same thing everyday. The girls and Louise were interrupted for a moment when the waiter brought over their drinks and almost spilled Ruth's order of a Tom Collins with extra fruit.

"Let me ask you this. Why do the medicine men let all the teenagers get preggers?" Ruth said to Louise. "Can't they make them wait till it's decent? It's so bad for the little kids to see."

"It's hormones," Abby said. "They're just hot and stupid. In the middle school, they've got a couple of 14-year-olds at watermelon size. I saw them yesterday at the cafeteria. Could you teach a girl like that?"

Louise said, "I know it's embarrassing to us — sex is a naughty subject. But these girls have to prove they're fertile before anyone will marry them."

"Oh, I get it," Abby said and laughed. "You're telling me they have a different morality." Then Abby laughed some more, but Ruth was only half listening. She had palmed one of Louise's half-smoked Benson & Hedges from the ashtray. She put the filter carefully up to her lips, so she could match her lipstick mark to Louise's.

"Are Seven and Sevens good?" Ruth asked Louise as she relit the cigarette.

Louise left the girls right after the one drink, and they imagined she was going right over to spend the night with Joe. She had no children, so she still had something to prove to him as far as they could tell. Over a couple more drinks with their T-bone dinners and the Cleaver's Special Drunk Dessert with a cup of decaf coffee, they discussed the merits of the leather handbags on sale down at the Sears outlet and what a body wave could do for Ruth. At closing, after a cocktail for the road, the girls drove down Courthouse Boulevard to the Wagon Master's Drive-Thru

Liquors where their faces were blue in the neon as they placed their order. By one a.m., the girls were already 15 miles down 187 away from Casa Grande. Abby had settled into the backseat with her corduroy car coat tucked over her shoulders. She had waved good-bye to the town's lights as they flickered out around Big Bend turn five miles back. Now there was only the pale glow across the sky like a painter's mistake in watercolors behind the stars and only Ruth to see it. At 70 miles an hour, she decided to use the middle line as a guide to keep ahold of the center.

An arroyo, filled last month during the rains, had splashed pebbles and debris inches deep across the low point in the road. Ruth sped up to spray the rocks back into the desert where they belong. She would have hummed to the radio if there was one. Instead she said to herself, "The car fishtails like a cod, and no one else is awake for hundreds of miles. And the road is running up to the sky."

Then she felt her chin sink into her chest of its own accord. She ought to spin the window handle to let in the colder, blacker air to wash over her. In her rearview mirror she smiled at the red afterglow of her taillights. It spread out like a cape wide enough to light in a purpley way a roadside shrine to the Virgin mounted on a pedestal of desert rocks and cement. There were four or so foot-tall crosses beneath it, a small forest, for the Indians that had died on this spot in the road. Ruth thought of swerving off the pavement into the next series of white sticks and knocking them down like dominoes. She thought she'd use the stuff for kindling. "I'd probably need Louise's jeep for this off-the-road work," she said out loud. Wouldn't Louise be just sick to find white splinters in her tires and front fender. She'd have me arrested for snubbing the Indians, she thought.

Ruth drove right past the St. Joseph's Well turn-off that went straight to the school and past to Sing-Sing. She wanted to see the Arch Stone in the hills six miles south of the dorms. It was supposed to be magical, and on full moon nights, the medicine men had secret ceremonies there, or so people said. Since tonight there were only stars and a quarter moon out, Ruth knew she'd be alone at Wedding Ring, as she called it. When the car stopped, Abby didn't even turn over in the backseat. She just let long, thin whistles out from behind her teeth. Lit up by the headlights was the female shape of the Arch, the water-washed stone eroded by an ancient ocean. It was the best thing Ruth had ever seen, and it arched around so much that its end was its beginning.

Ruth opened the trunk and took out her bottle. She liked tearing the paper tape on the cap that meant it was not a tainted bottle. She took a long swallow, so she could climb the hill to the inside of the Ring in her high heels. At the top, she found the black marks of a fire but nothing more. She looked around on the ground for more evidence of visitors. Then she straightened up and planted her feet to straddle the floor of the curve. Like Moses calling down the Plagues, she lifted her arms up. What can I do for a sacrifice, she thought. Ruth put her thumb to the lip of the bottle and splashed from one end of the bottom half of the Ring to the other. "Spirits. Spirits, send me home," she called to nobody. She had another drink but felt more sober and silly after what she had done. I guess I'm ready to climb down, she thought. On the way, she slid three yards and tore two big holes in her nylons and scraped the inside of her right elbow. Maybe this wasn't a good place for wishes. At the car, Abby was half-awake and asked Ruth to take her home.

Ruth felt a blush on her neck and shoulders because maybe Abby had seen her. But nothing had really happened yet. Ruth didn't need to wait around all night to recognize when she'd been overlooked in her wishes. She got in the car, and even when she was backing out, she refused to glance back to the Ring. She swung off the dirt road, then remembered to put on her brights.

Faraway in the light on the highway's white line, there was a seven foot long rattler. She slowed down and twisted the wheel far to the right, so she could hit him on the diagonal. Every once in a while, she and Abby had gone out looking for snakes to run over, but nothing like this monster had she ever seen before. As she hit it, the car rolled sideways like a boat in disturbed water. Ruth liked the hollow cracking sound that was as satisfying as the noise dry wood makes when it snaps over a knee. She hoped Abby might wake up again, so she could show her what she'd done. Ruth backed up to see the silvery mess and a last flicker of nerves all by herself.

By Monday all the villages had heard about the snake. Thirty or more parents had come to take their kids out of class for a while. The teachers always called those parents who were so quick to judge, the traditionals. No one had known what exactly had happened or who had done it; but as one of the fathers tried to explain, they believed the misfortune of the snake was not a good sign.

A week later when everything was normal again, Miss Morris got mad at George for being one hour late to school and for being so filthy. She thought she recognized a guilty look on him as he stood in the doorway for a few minutes with his socks pulled out from his toes and his shoes tucked under his arms. Because of his shaven head, he looked like a miniature soldier with a camouflaged face. "Come here," Miss Morris commanded. "How did you get dirt on your forehead?"

George moved over to her, but refused to look at her, especially when she tried to lift his chin. His skull seemed a fragile, perfect oval — an egg with raw contents. "Squirm-worm, look at me," she said.

Suddenly George relaxed and oozed through her hold on his wrist. He backed toward the door with one sneaker in each hand and glared at her face. She felt a curse form in his icy eyes, and she didn't feel she could look to any of the other children in the class of his allies. He was gone in a breath. She ran after him but felt embarrassed by her breasts bouncing rubbery from side to side while she chased him down the hallway. She caught him by the shirt three steps from the front door.

"I'll make you better," she said as she tried to comfort him while taking him back to the room. It was the only thing she could think of saying because there was no way for him to win.

Back by the sink, she held him as she mopped the soapy water away from his eyes. He was not physically fighting her anymore. But as he lay in her arms, his agitation felt as warm as a fever to her and just as contagious. She imagined they might both take a chill by this evening. Even the dry paper towel crushed in her palm was damp.

None of her other children would say another word to her all day long. She missed her usual coffee in the lounge fifth hour, and when Abby stuck her head in, just to check, Ruth shook her head no. She let the kids look at magazines from the cut-out picture pile, and she spent the day writing out lesson plans in the two-by-two-inch boxes that filled the official schedule book. She could go home then, and get good and sick. For the last 15 minutes of class, Ruth let her kids go out to the playground to where twisted and bent metal poles hunched in the dirt lot. At exactly 2:50, she left school an hour and some minutes before her contract allowed her to leave the classroom. She got home before anyone could have seen her, and she locked both locks on her front door. After pulling the drapes, she mixed some bourbon into her weak ice tea. She needed to keep her mind as busy as she could make it. Maybe she could redecorate her kitchen. By tomorrow, everyone would have heard. She imagined the empty desks which would be all she'd have left in her classroom. What had she ruined?

Cleanliness is next to Godliness. Silence is Golden. It's the early bird who catches the worm. It's the pot calling the kettle black. She wanted to convince herself she knew all she had to know to teach. She got up to wash her hands in the kitchen and was dizzy enough to lay her head on the cool white porcelain divider between the sinks. She took a dampened tea towel back with her to the couch and wiped it across her widow's peak. As she fumbled with the phone to dial the office to make an excuse for tomorrow, she lay sideways on the couch and willed her sickness to be real.

By five p.m., the sun was dancing on the tips of the Santa Rose Mountains, and she was drunk. She had made the bed after her nap, taken out the garbage, and now she was ready to go. She locked her front door and threw the key into the green painted pebbles of her yard. She took two swallows of her bourbon straight from the bottle before she could unlock her car. She got in and headed away from Casa Grande toward Yuma or maybe Mexico.

The sunset was boiling orange in her eyes after 20 miles and made black stars shoot across her sight. The road was getting narrower and narrower and would be littered with the carcasses of anything she could possibly meet. She was wiping her vision clear as she ran off the road and skidded round and round. She was the eye of a hurricane, and time grew slower and slower wherever she was. Ruth sat in her car in a wash facing the mountains, away from the road. With her eyelids blinking, she could hear the animals in the mesquite, and she could feel the animals crawling among the boulders on the mountains. She opened her eyes wide to see that the mountains all had notches as the sky blazed behind them, and they were only two dimensions. Then she rolled her head from side to side, and notches became mouths that would sing to the Indians.

Contributors

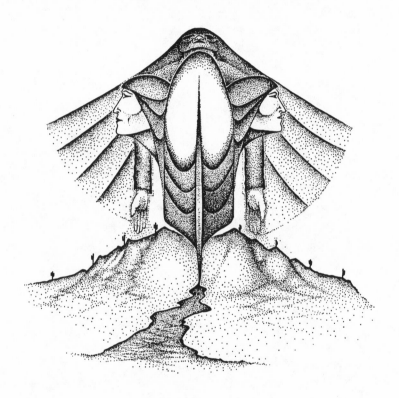

Antone, Barbara A.

Barbara A. Antone, a Quechan, was born and raised on the Ft. Yuma Indian Reservation but lived off-reservation in the Phoenix metropolitan area for nearly eight years. She says of herself, "I still live by the traditional values of the Quechan people. I am teaching my children to be bi-lingual and to walk forward and cross over a bridge which has made men share their cross-cultural life. I love to paint and draw. I also do beadwork. I sing the Mohave Bird Songs with my husband who is a traditional singer. I also dance the Bird Dances." Antone's literary experience also includes assisting Byrd Baylor in one of her books of children's short stories, published in the early 1970s.

Archambault, Avis

Avis Archambault, a Lakota-Gros Ventre, was born at Ft. Belknap, Montana. Her education, a B.F.A. in Art and a M.A. in Humanities (Dance) included studies in France. She has taught at college/university levels in the areas of art/dance/humanities and has an extensive background in dance as a performer/choreographer in her own modern dance troupe, "Mixed Company." Archambault is currently director of "Talking Circle" project, a native-therapeutic model, using women/youth/families in an Arizona urban Indian center.

She explains, "At the very heart of my identity, I would say that I am a Lakota-Gros Ventre woman, a Pipe-Carrier for my people. I've lived on and off the reservation, and my home is Ft. Belknap, Montana. Yet, I have come to respect and appreciate the power of this desert country. Arizona has become my second home and holds an integral place in my learning."

Aroniawenrate / Peter Blue Cloud

Aroniawenrate / Peter Blue Cloud is of the Mohawk Nation, Turtle Clan at Kahnawake. He has had four books published and edited several anthologies. Of his current work he says, "I am busy painting and carving mindscapes across the panels of my imagination. The enclosed poem began happening as I crossed from California into Arizona. I have taken frequent trips through the Southwest, and though a northeastern, cold-weather Indian, the Southwest moves me as few other areas do."

Barnes, Jim

Jim Barnes, of Choctaw-Welsh heritage, edits the *Chariton Review* at Northeast Missouri State University. His most recent books of poetry are *The American Book of the Dead* (University of Illinois Press) and *A Season of Loss* (Purdue University Press). His association with Arizona comes from having driven through it many times on his way to and from Oregon, his adopted home. About his poem he says, "On my first trip through Arizona, in 1951, I puzzled for a long while over the many small, white crosses dotting the shoulders of Route 66."

Bruchac, Joseph

Joseph Bruchac is St. Francis Abenaki on his mother's side of the family, and he was raised by his maternal grandparents in the Adirondack foothills near the town of Saratoga Springs — where his grandfather used to sell his handmade ash-splint baskets to the tourists. He was born in 1942 and has been exploring the Abenaki side of his heritage in his writing since his teen-age years.

He has visited Arizona five times to do workshops in the prisons, readings of his own work, and interviews with Native American poets. He has also published work by a number of Arizona Indian writers in such anthologies as *Songs From This Earth on Turtle's Back* and *Light From Another Country*. "My continued contact throughout the years with Arizona Indian people has been a deep influence," he notes.

He writes poetry, fiction, essays, and retellings of traditional myths and legends (Abenaki and Iroquois). His published books include *Near the Mountains, Selected Poems* (1987), *Iroquoise Stories* (1985) and a collection of interviews with Native American poets, *Survival This Way* (1987).

Butler, Leonard G.

Leonard G. Butler is a full-blooded Navajo. In his childhood, he lived in the Tuba City, Cameron, and Gray Mountain areas of the reservation in Arizona. At the age of six, he went to live with a foster family in Salt Lake City, Utah, where he went to school and lived for about 14 years. He returned to the reservation when he was 19 years old and just recently moved to live in Flagstaff, Arizona.

About his current life, he says, "I have chosen law enforcement as a career and have worked in various areas of the reservation. At the present time I am employed as a police officer with the Northern Arizona University Police Department."

Cling, Marvin

Marvin Cling, a Navajo Indian, currently resides in the northern part of Arizona at Shonto which is close to Navajo Mountain. He graduated from Monument Valley High School and attended the University of Arizona for two years.

About his writing, he says, "I have been living on the Navajo Indian Reservation for 17 years. I plan to complete a manuscript on certain

Navajo clan origins and the lores that describe them. The poem, 'The New Moon,' is about a Navajo medicine man who is a skin walker, also known as a Navajo werewolf."

Cooley, Benjamin

Benjamin Cooley is a Navajo, age 38, from Leupp, Arizona. "My writings are basically short stories and poetry. Though I am hopeful of becoming a writer someday, I consider it a hobby now," he explains.

Crank, Dan L.

Dan L. Crank is a Navajo Indian currently residing at Dennehotso, Arizona on the Navajo Reservation. He attended schools and lived on and off the reservation for several years. He received a Bachelor of Arts degree in Education from the University of Arizona, 1978.

He explains, "Currently, I work with Navajo high school students, and enjoy providing them with experiences I encountered when I lived in the cities. In my free time I write short stories and poetry and photograph scenes around my home area. I like to think I specialize in moody Monument Valley scenes." His photos and one short story have been published in various issues of *Maazo Magazine*.

Curtis, Jefferson L.

Jefferson L. Curtis, a Navajo, was born on August 2, 1971. Of himself, he says, "My hobbies would probably be student athletic training, drawing and collecting magazines. I don't write that much, only draw more than write. I like high school a lot, because I learn different things every day."

Forbes, Jack D.

Jack D. Forbes is of Powhatoan and Delaware background. About his connection to Arizona, he writes, "I have been in and out of Arizona often since the 1950s, mostly to visit Indian reservations for conferences or just for exploration. I also have had a lot of relations living in Arizona, especially Tucson. My father-in-law is buried in Tucson and my sister-in-law is a student at the University of Arizona."

George, Dorothy T.

Dorothy T. George is a Hopi Indian and a lifetime resident of Arizona. She says, "I have not done too much writing, except for literature classes. I am a working mother with three grown children and two in school, a son in high school and a daughter in mid-school."

Hail, Raven

Raven Hail, Cherokee, was born on an oil lease north of Dewey, Oklahoma, and lived on her mother's Cherokee Land Allotment near Welch, Oklahoma as a child. She attended Oklahoma State University, Stillwater, Oklahoma, and Southern Methodist University, Dallas, Texas.

Her articles and poems have appeared in *The Cherokee Advocate, The Cherokee Nation News, Nimrod, Cimarron Review, Translation, The State, Quetzal, Gray Day, Tosan, Indian Voice, The Blue Cloud Quarterly, Daybreak, The Wayside Quarterly, An American Indian Anthology, Lacuna, Poetry Dallas, The Remembered Earth, The Texas Anthology, The Herb Quarterly,* and *Bestways Magazine.* Her published works include *The Pleiades Stones, Windsong, Native American Foods* and *The Raven Speaks.*

Harjo, Joy

Joy Harjo was born in Tulsa, Oklahoma in 1951 and is a member of the Creek Tribe. She received her M.F.A. in Creative Writing from the Iowa Writers Workshop at the University of Iowa in 1978. She also attended the Anthropology Film Center in Santa Fe. She has published three books of poetry including *She Had Some Horses* (Thunder's Mouth Press) and *Secrets From the Center of the World.* A collaboration with photographer/astronomer Stephen Strom was released Fall, 1989 from University of Arizona Press. She is Associate Professor in the Department of English at the University of Arizona, Tucson and is on the Board of Directors for the Native American Public Broadcasting Consortium. She is also poetry editor for *High Plains Literary Review.* She was a dramatic screenwriter for Silvercloud Video Productions. She is at work on three other projects including a fourth book of poetry, and plays the soprano saxophone.

Hendricks, Adrian

Adrian Hendricks is Pima and Papago and has been working with his art since he was a small boy. Currently he is a senioir at Arizona State University, where he is majoring in history. After graduation he hopes to return to Sacaton to teach and continue with his art, "as long as I don't get tired of it."

To prepare the art work for this anthology Adrian read the complete manuscript and made sketches and final pen and ink drawings for those pieces that "made him think."

Henson, Lance

Lance Henson is a Cheyenne poet who was raised and still lives in his grandparent's home built on traditional Cheyenne campgrounds near

Calumet, Oklahoma. He is an ex-Marine, member of the Black Belt Karate Association, the Cheyenne Dog Warrior Society and the Native American Church. He has a B.A. in English and an M.A. degree in Creative Writing.

His poetry has been published in most major anthologies of Native American literature including, *Carriers of the Dream Wheel, Voices of the Rainbow, The Remembered Earth, The Clouds Threw This Light,* and *Songs From This Earth on Turtle's Back.* In addition, he has published ten books of poetry including *Keeper of Arrows, Naming the Dark, Buffalo Marrow on Black, In A Dark Mist,* and *A Circling Remembrance.*

He is a lecturer, workshop teacher and poet-in-residence and has toured both the United States and Europe with his poetry.

Inoj / Joan A. Torralba

Joan A. Torralba has been writing for the past 15 years as a hobby. She is a member of the Kiowa Indian Tribe of Oklahoma, but has been living on the Hopi Reservation for the past two years.

She explains, "The history and traditions of the Hopi people are quite fascinating. One day as I was sitting in my car at Second Mesa store, I observed the rain falling and thought how precious water is to this area. I watched low hanging clouds move up and over Second Mesa in the distance." From this experience she decided to write the poem, "Hopiland."

Jackson, Genevieve

Genevieve Jackson is a full-blooded Navajo and was born in Fort Defiance, Arizona. She still maintains a house there. She explains, "Although I reside in Kirtland, New Mexico, I do not consider it my home, merely a place to live for easier access to my place of employment."

She earned her B.S. degree in Elementary Education with a minor in Bilingual Education and a M.A. in Educational Administration from the University of New Mexico.

About her work she says, "I have worked with Central Consolidated School District #22 in Shiprock, New Mexico for ten years as a teacher, oral language monitor and a principal. I enjoy my job very much. I also enjoy writing, but I don't have much time to devote to it."

Jackson, Valerie

Valerie Jackson is currently majoring in English at Arizona State University where she has been a student since 1983. She is a member of the Crow Tribe from southeastern Montana, and she has lived in Tempe, Arizona for four years with her sons Joshua and Spencer White Shirt.

Kaulaity, Marlinda

Marlinda Kaulaity is a Navajo who resides in Fort Defiance, Arizona on the Navajo Reservation. Of Arizona she says, "I have lived here since I was five years old. My clan people are from Whitecone, Arizona where my 'true roots' are. Arizona is the only home I know."

She is a 1979 graduate of Arizona State University, and currently she is teaching English and Native American Literature at Window Rock High School in Fort Defiance where she has been for eight years.

Keams, Geri

Geri Keams grew up on the Navajo Nation in the small community of Castle Buttes, Arizona. The oldest of nine brothers and sisters, she was raised and greatly influenced by her grandmother who is a traditional Navajo rug weaver.

She recalls, "At a young age, I was taught the importance of remembering and carrying on the ancient tribal stories and chants. Most Navajos had no radio or television when I was growing up; storytelling was both a way to entertain and to educate the young people. I remembered what my grandmother taught me."

She graduated from the University of Arizona in 1978 with a degree in drama education and toured with the Native American Theatre Ensemble based in New York City. There she was a major influence in a theatrical production based on the creation myth of the Navajo.

Since then, Geri has acted in TV and feature films; she played a leading role in the Clint Eastwood film, "The Outlaw Josey Wales." She has traveled throughout the U.S. and Europe sharing her stories, poems and chants.

Kenny, Maurice

Maurice Kenny was born in 1929 between the St. Lawrence and Black Rivers. He currently lives in Saranac Lake of the Adirondack Mountains in New York, where he co-edits the poetry journal *Contact/11* with J.G. Gosciak. He is also the publisher of Strawberry Press. Besides the collection in *Between Two Rivers*, Mr. Kenny is the author of *Is Summer This Bear* (1985), *Greyhounding This America* (1986), *Rain and Other Fictions* (1985), and a collection of historical essays, *Roman Nose and Other Essays* (1986). His work appears in *North American Poetry* (Harper & Row), *Earth Power Coming* (Navajo Community College Press), *Wab Kon Tab* (International Publishers), *Art Against Apartheid* (Ikon), and *I Tell You Now: Autobiographies of Native American Writers* (University of Nebraska). He edited *Wounds Beneath The Flesh* (*Blue Cloud Quarterly,* 1983). In 1984, he received the prestigious American Book Award for *The Mama Poems*

(White Pine Press). Of his work and life he says, "I am committed to the earth and the past: to tradition and the future. I am committed to people and poetry." He is currently at work on a new collection of persona poems, *Tekonwatonti, Molly Brant: Poems of War.*

Link, Virgil

Virgil Link holds a degree in Journalism/Public Relations from Northern Arizona University. He is presently living on the San Carlos Reservation and is working at Globe High School as a student attendance officer. He says, "I hope to teach either Journalism or English whenever San Carlos constructs its high school within the next years."

Lomawywesa / Michael Kabotie

Lomawywesa/Michael Kabotie artist, jeweler and poet was born in 1942 in the Hopi Indian village of Shungopavi in Arizona. Lomawywesa is a member of the Snow/Water Clan of his people and is active in Hopi traditional and ceremonial activity. He received his education at the Hopi High School and graduated from Haskell Institute in Lawrence, Kansas in 1961. When Lomawywesa attended the University of Arizona College of Engineering he was encouraged by friends to paint. He found that he was happier painting and in 1966 he held his first one-man show at the Heard Museum, Phoenix, Arizona. Since then he has exhibited widely and won a number of awards throughout the country. In 1987 the University of California, Los Angeles published a collection of his poems titled *Migration Tears; Poems about Transitions.* About his work, Lomawywesa says, "The arts have always been an integral part of my life. It is through the arts that I capture and share the values of people's spirituality, agonies, contradictions, happiness and through the arts that I clarify my fears, passions, joys; my birth and death."

Louis, Adrian C.

Adrian C. Louis is a native Nevadan and has, at various times, resided in Phoenix, Flagstaff and Tucson. He is an enrolled Northern Paiute Indian and has edited four different tribal newspapers. He is a founder of the Native American Press Association and has been teaching English at Oglala Lakota College on the Pine Ridge Reservation of South Dakota since 1984. His fourth collection of poems, *Fire Water World*, was published by West End Press in January, 1989.

Molina-Whillock, Maria Valenzuela

Maria (Mercy) Valenzuela Molina-Whillock was born and raised in Marana, Arizona, a farming community 25 miles northwest of Tucson.

She explains, "My grandparents and uncles were warriors during the Yaqui's fight to maintain tribal lands in the early 1900's against the Mexican government and were well known religious leaders and medicine people among Yaquis in Tucson and Marana." Raised in the traditional Yaqui lifestyle she spent her early years in the Yaqui religious ceremonies and was taught the history and language of her people.

She attended the University of Arizona, College of Business Administration and Pima Community College working towards a degree in Public Administration. Her work has always focused on advocacy for Indian participation in program and government policy at local, state and national levels.

Mercy Molina-Whillock was one of the first Yaqui community organizers led by Anselmo Valencia to found the Pascua Yaqui Association.

Morris, Irvin

Irvin Morris is a full blood Navajo, born and raised on the reservation. He says, "What I am and what I write about arises out of that experience. I am, for the most part, self-taught. This despite the fact that I have attended Navajo Community College and the University of New Mexico. I hope to one day resume my formal training. I have been published in a quarterly publication, *Maazo Magazine*, so I know I have interesting things to say." He is from the northern part of the state and currently resides in Fort Defiance.

Nakai, Tyra

Tyra Nakai is 16 years old from northern Arizona. She describes herself by saying, "I love to play sports, draw and write poetry. I have never been published. My father is Navajo, my mother is Anglo. I was born in Fort Defiance and moved away a couple of months after. Now I have come back after 16 years."

Perea, Robert L.

Robert L. Perea was born in Wheatland, Wyoming on January 5, 1946. "My mother is Oglala Sioux and my father is Mexican-American," he explains, "I spent two years in the Peace Corps in Venezuela as a coach (1971-1973), two years in the U.S. Army — year in Vietnam — as a radio operator, seven years at the Phoenix Indian School (1981-1988)." He is currently on the staff of Central Arizona Community College.

His short stories have been published mostly in Native American and Chicano literary journals and anthologies. All his stories have been about the Vietnam War, except for one story about his Indian grandmother published in *Earth Power Coming* edited by Simon Ortiz. Commenting on "The Hot Desert Breeze: A Children's Story," he says, "Being a 'husband' isn't worth the effort . . . being a 'father' is."

Salisbury, Ralph

Ralph Salisbury's life until he turned 18 and went into the Air Force, was about as close to the old days as possible — hunting, planting and finding spirit-awareness in Nature — even though he grew up in Iowa. Since then, he has worked as a farm laborer, construction worker, janitor, photographer, journalist, university professor, literary editor, fiction writer and poet. Of his poems and fiction, he says, "I try to speak for people who have to struggle hard for any sense of dignity, well-being and beauty in their lives. I am one of them."

His poems and stories have appeared in many magazines and anthologies in England, Canada and the U.S. His books are *Ghost Grapefruit and Other Poets* (Ithaca House), *Pointing At The Rainbow* (Blue Cloud Press), *Spirit Beast Chant* (Blue Cloud Press) and *Going to the Water: Poems of a Cherokee Heritage* (Pacific Books). He is a professor of English at the University of Oregon and an editor of an anthology of contemporary Native American writing, *The Nation Within*, from Outrigger Publishers, New Zealand.

Sanchez, Gabriella

Gabriella (Gala) Sanchez is the 13-year-old daughter of a Pima Indian mother and a Pueblo Indian father. Her family came to the Salt River Community approximately ten years ago. She is a seventh grader at Kino Jr. High School in Mesa, Arizona.

Gala lives with her mother and two sisters in what she calls a modern environment. She says, "My mother's tribe is losing some of their culture, but my father's people still have many of their old customs and dances, and language in their village in New Mexico. My father was really frightened as a boy when he first went into town. He had been very protected in his small village."

Gala was born in Phoenix and has lived all of her live in Arizona.

Sands, Kathleen Mullen

Kathleen Mullen Sands is a professor in the Department of English at Arizona State University where she teaches American Indian literatures, folklore, and literatures of the American West. She is the co-author of *American Indian Women Telling Their Lives* (University of Nebraska Press, 1984) and editor of *Autobiography of a Yaqui Poet* (University of Arizona Press, 1980) and *People of Pascua* (University of

Arizona Press, 1988). She has published articles on American Indian traditional and contemporary literatures in *American Indian Quarterly, American Indian Culture and Research Journal, American Quarterly,* and *Studies in American Indian Literatures.* She has also written chapters for several critical anthologies on American Indian literatures and has served as the president of the Association for the Study of American Indian Literatures.

Smith, R.T.

R.T. Smith, a Tuscaroran, says of his experiences in the Southwest, "Although I ranged nomadic about the Southwest this past summer, I was stationed at the Wurlitzer Foundation in New Mexico, and in that vicinity I began to explore the ruins, both excavated and unexcavated, of the Mesa Verdean and Chacoan Anasazi, one of the early tribes to wrest life (and to thrive, momentarily) in the deserts. Although my tribal affiliation is strictly eastern, I felt the ripple of inescapable recognition in the caves, the petroglyphs, the sherds and ladders and tumbled walls. The more I walked over those ruins and touched what the signs said not to, the more I felt that writing is kin to archaeology. We dig beneath the rubble of the personality to the deeper, communal impulses and patterns, and we reconstruct, for a small space, a chant, a dance, a fetish that lends both comfort and challenge to our lives. Like the Anasazi, we build for immediate utility, but we also build work we hope will last."

Tallmountain, Mary

Mary Tallmountain is an Athabascan/Koyukon/Celtic woman who was born in the territory of Alaska in 1918. Explaining how she came to Arizona she says, "I was separated by adoption from my parents in 1924, and lost touch with my father, Clem Stroupe, but over 50 years later, I found him retired from the Air Force, 86 years old, and living in Sunnyslope, Arizona. He grew ill; I went to Phoenix and helped him get well. He lived for two years happily, and succumbed to his cancer at 88.

The desert mesmerized me, and I fell in love with the summer storms. I ran around and around Dad's cabin, shrieking with delight in the wind, seeing every step of the living storm approaching, and savoring the marvelous congruence of terror and joy — the energies of the storm itself."

During her time in Arizona, she wrote some and worked extensively on a novel concerning the effects of the adoption of children into a separate culture. "Wild Birds Flying" is the outcome of her years in Arizona.

Wilson, Cynthia

Cynde Wilson, a Seminole, has spent most of her life in Arizona where she completed a M.A. degree at Arizona State University and a M.F.A. degree in creative writing from the University of Arizona. She and her husband lived in Japan for four years where she taught English and studied Japanese dance and calligraphy. She is both a poet and fiction writer and has taught in the Arizona Arts Commission Poetry-in-the-Schools Program with particular interest in working with students in reservation schools.

Wolf, Phyllis

Phyllis Wolf is an Assiniboine-Ojibway, who received both her undergraduate and graduate degrees in Arizona, and wrote her first poems there. She currently resides in California and explains why, "I developed a great chili quiche in Arizona, was mistaken for a Papago, and had to move."

Zillioux, Mike Medicine Horse

Mike Medicine Horse Zillioux says of himself simply, "I am Pima, Sioux and Cheyenne and enrolled at Gila River."